A Tale of a Tub by Ben Jonson

A COMEDY. From the 1640 folio.

Benjamin "Ben" Jonson was born in June, 1572. A contemporary of William Shakespeare, he is best known for his satirical plays; Volpone, The Alchemist, and Bartholomew Fair, and his equally accomplished lyric poems.

A man of vast reading and a seemingly insatiable appetite for controversy, including time in jail and a penchant for switching faiths, Jonson had an unparalleled breadth of influence on Jacobean and Caroline playwrights and poets.

In 1616 Jonson was appointed by King James I to receive a yearly pension of £60 to become what is recognised as the first official Poet Laureate.

He died on the 6th of August, 1637 at Westminster and is buried in the north aisle of the nave at Westminster Abbey.

A master of both playwriting and poetry his reputation continues to endure and reach a new audience with each succeeding generation.

Index of Contents

PROLOGUE

No State-affairs, nor any politick Club,
Pretend we in our Tale, here, of a Tub:
But acts of Clowns and Constables, to day
Stuff out the Scenes of our ridiculous Play.
A Coopers wit, or some such busie Spark,
Illumining the high Constable, and his Clerk.
And all the Neighbour-hood, from old Records,
Of antick Proverbs, drawn from Whitson-Lords.
And their Authorities, at Wakes and Ales,
With Country precedents, and old Wives Tales;
We bring you now, to shew what different things
The Cotes of Clowns, are from the Courts of Kings.

The PERSONS that ACT

CHANON HUGH,	Vicar of Pancrass, and Captain Thums.
SQUIRE TUB,	Of Totten-Court, or Squire Tripoly.

BASKET - HILTS,	His Man, and Governor.
JUST. PREAMBLE,	Of Maribone, alias Bramble.
MILES METAPHOR,	His Clerk.
Lady TUB,	Of Totten, the Squire's Mother.
POL-MARTEN,	Her Huisher: Dido Wisp her Woman.
TOBIE TURFE	High Constable of Kentish Town.
Da. SIBIL TURFE,	His Wife.
Mrs. AWDREY TURFE	Their Daughter the Bride.
JOHN CLAY	Of Kilborn Tile-maker, the appointed Bride Groom.
IN-AND-IN MEDLAY	Of Islington, Cooper and Headborough.
RASI. CLENCH	Of Hamsted, Farrier, and petty Constable.
TO-PAN	Tinker, or Mettal-man of Belsise, Thirdborough.
D'OGE SCRIBEN	Of Chalcot, the great writer.
BALL PUPPY	The high Constable's Man.
FATHER ROSIN,	The Minstrel, and his two Boys.
JONE, JOYCE, }	
MADGE, PARNEL, }	Maids of the Bridal
GRISEL, KATE, }	
BLACK JACK,	The Lady Tub's Butler.
Two GROOMS.	

The SCENE - FINSBURY-HUNDRED.

ACT I. SCENE I

SIR HUGH, TUB, HILTS.

SIR HUGH - Now o' my Faith, Old Bishop Valentine,
You ha' brought us nipping weather: Februere
Doth cut and shear; your day, and Diocess
Are very cold. All your Parishioners;
As well your Layicks, as your Quiristers,
Had need to keep to their warm Feather-beds,
If they be sped of Loves: this is no season,
To seek new Makes in; though Sir Hugh of Pancrace,
Be hither come to Totten, on intelligence,
To the young Lord o' the Mannor, Squire Tripoly,
On such an Errand as a Mistris is.
What, Squire! I say? Tub, part of
Sir Hugh's dialogue I should call him too:
Sir Peter Tub was his Father, a Salt-petre-man;
Who left his Mother, Lady Tub of Totten-
Court, here, to revel, and keep open House in;
With the young Squire her Son, and's Governour Basket-
Hilts, both by Sword and Dagger: Domine,
Armiger Tub, Squire Tripoly, Expergiscere.
I dare not call alood, lest heshe should hear me:
And think I conjur'd up the Spirit, her Son,

In Priests-lack-Latine: O she is jealous
Of all Mankind for him.

TUB - Chanon, i'stis't you?

[At the Windor.

SIR HUGH - The Vicar of Pancrace, Squire Tub! wa' hoh!

TUB - I come, I stoop unto the call; Sir Hugh!

[He comes down in his Night-Gown.

SIR HUGH - He knows my lure is from his Love: fair Awdrey,
Th'high Constables Daughter of Kentish-Town, here, Mr.
Tobias Turfe.

TUB - What news of him?

SIR HUGH - He has wak'd me
An hour before I would, Sir. And my duty
To the young Worship of Totten-Court, Squire Tripoly;
Who hath my heart, as I have his: your Mrs.
Is to be made away from you, this morning,
Saint Valentines day: there are a knot of Clowns,
The Counsel of Finsbury, so they are y-styl'd,
Met at her Fathers; all the wise o' th' hundred;
Old BasiRasi Clench of Hamsted, petty Constable;
In-and-In Medlay, Cooper of Islington,
And Headborough; with loud To-Pan, the Tinker,
Or Metal-man of Belsise, the Third-borough:
And D'ogenes Scriben, the great Writer of Chalcot.

TUB - And why all these?

SIR HUGH - Sir, to conclude in Counsel,
A Husband, or a Make for Mrs. Awdrey;
Whom they have nam'd, and prick'd down, Clay of Kilborn,
A tough young fellow, and a Tile-maker.

TUB - And what must he do?

SIR HUGH - Cover her, they say:
And keep her warm, Sir: Mrs. Awdrey Turfe,
Last night did draw him for her Valentine;
Which chance, it hath so taken her Father and Mother,
(Because themselves drew so, on Valentine's Eve
Was thirty year) as they will have her married
To day by any means; they have sent a Messenger
To Kilborn, post, for Clay; which when I knew,
I posted with the like to worshipful Tripoly,

The Squire of Totten: and my advise to cross it.

TUB - What is't, Sir Hugh?

SIR HUGH - Where is your Governour Hilts?
Basquet must do it.

TUB - Basquet shall be call'd:
Hilts, can you see to rise?

HILTS - Cham not blind, Sir,
With too much light.

TUB - Open your t'other Eye,
And view if it be day.

HILTS - Che can spy that
At's little a hole as another, through a Milstone.

TUB - He will ha' the last word, though he talk Bilke for't.

SIR HUGH - Bilke? what's that?

TUB - Why, nothing, a word signifying
Nothing; and borrow'd here to express nothing.

SIR HUGH - A fine device!

TUB - Yes, till we hear a finer.
What's your device now, Chanon Hugh?

SIR HUGH - In private.
Lend it your Ear; I will not trust the Air with it;
Or scarce my Shirt; my Cassock sha' not know it;
If I thought it did, I'll burn it.

TUB - That's the way,
You ha' thought to get a new one, Hugh: Is't worth it?
Let's hear it first.

[They whisper.

SIR HUGH - Then hearken, and receive it.
This 'tis, Sir, do you relish it?

TUB - If Hilts
Be close enough to carry it; there's all.

[HILTS enters, and walks by, making himself ready,

HILTS - It i' no Sand? nor Butter-milk? If't be,

Ich'am no Zive, or Watring-pot, to draw
Knots i' your 'casions. If you trust me, zo:
If not, praform it your zelves. Cham no Man's Wife,
But resolute Hilts: you'll vind me i' the Buttry.

TUB - A testy Clown: but a tender Clown, as wooll:
And melting as the Weather in a Thaw:
He'll weep you, like all April: But he'ull roar you,
Like middle March afore: He will be as mellow,
And tipsie too, as October: And as grave,
And bound up like a Frost (with the new year)
In January; as rigid as he is rustick.

SIR HUGH - You know his Nature, and describe it well;
I'll leave him to your fashioning.

TUB - Stay, Sir Hugh;
Take a good Angel with you, for your Guide:
And let this guard you homeward, as the blessing,
To our device.

SIR HUGH - I thank you Squires Worship,
Most humbly (for the next, for this I am sure of.)

[The SQUIRE goes off.

O for a Quire of these Voices, now,
To chime in a Man's Pocket, and cry chink!
One doth not chirp: it makes no harmony.
Grave Justice Bramble, next must contribute;
His Charity must offer at this Wedding:
I'll bid more to the Bason, and the Bride-Ale;
Although but one can bear away the Bride.
I smile to think how like a Lottery
These Weddings are. Clay hath her in possession;
The Squire he hopes to circumvent the Tile-Kill:
And now, if Justice Bramble do come off,
'Tis two to one but Tub may lose his bottom.

ACT I. SCENE II

CLENCH, MEDLAY, SCRIBEN, TO-PAN, PUPPY.

CLENCH - Why, 'tis thirty year, e'en as this day now,
Zin Valentine's day, of all days kursin'd, look you;
And the zame day o' the Month, as this Zin Valentine,
Or I am vowly deceiv'd.

MEDLAY - That our High Constable,

Mr. Tobias Turfe, and his Dame were married.
I think you are right. But what was that Zin Valentine?
Did you ever know 'um, Good-man Clench?

CLENCH - Zin Valentine,
He was a deadly Zin, and dwelt at High-gate,
As I have heard; but 'twas avore my time:
He was a Cooper too, as you are, Medlay,
An' In-an-In: A woundy brag young vellow:
As th' port went o' hun then, and i' those days.

SCRIBEN - Did he not write his Name, Sim Valentine?
Vor I have met no Sin in Finsbury Books;
And yet I have writ 'em six or seven times over.

TO-PAN - O' you mun look for the Nine deadly Sims,
I' the Church-books, D'oge; not the high Constables;
Nor i' the Counties: Zure, that same Zin Valentine,
He was a stately Zin: an' he were a Zin,
And kept brave house.

CLENCH - At the Cock and Hen in High-gate.
You ha' 'fresh'd my rememory well in't! neighbour Pan:
He had a Place in last King Harry's time,
Of sorting all the young Couples; joyning 'em,
And putting 'em together; which is yet
Praform'd, as on his day—Zin Valentine;
As being the Zin o' the Shire, or the whole County:
I am old Rivet still, and bear a Brain,
The Clench, the Varrier, and true Leach of Hamsted.

TO-PAN - You are a shrewd Antiquity, neighbour Clench!
And a great Guide to all the Parishes!
The very Bell-weather of the Hundred, here,
As I may zay. Mr. Tobias Turfe,
High Constable, would not miss you, for a Score on us,
When he doe'scourse of the great Charty to us.

PUPPY - What's that, a Horse? Can 'scourse nought but a Horse?
I ne're read o' hun, and that in Smith-veld Charty:
I' the old Fabians Chronicles: nor I think
In any new. He may be a Giant there,
For ought I know.

SCRIBEN - You should do well to study
Records, Fellow Ball, both Law and Poetry.

PUPPY - Why, all's but writing, and reading, is it Scriben?
An't be any more, it's meer cheating zure.
Vlat cheating: all your Law, and Poets too.

TO-PAN - Mr. High Constable comes.

PUPPY - I'll zay't avore 'hun.

TURFE, CLENCH, MEDLAY, SCRIBEN, PUPPY, TO-PAN.

TURFE - What's that makes you all so merry, and loud, Sirs, ha?
I could ha' heard you to my privy walk.

CLENCH - A Contervarsie 'twixt your two learn'd Men here:
Annibal Puppy says, that Law and Poetry
Are both flat cheating; All's but writing and reading,
He says, be't Verse or Prose.

TURFE - I think in conzience,
He do' zay true? Who is't do thwart 'un, ha?

MEDLAY - Why, my Friend Scriben, and't please your
Worship.

TURFE - Who, D'oge? my D'ogenes? a great Writer, marry!
He'll vace me down, me my self sometimes,
That Verse goes upon Veet, as you and I do:
But I can gi' 'un the hearing; zit me down,
And laugh at 'un; and to my self conclude,
The greatest Clerks are not the wisest Men
Ever. Here they' re both! What, Sirs, disputing,
And holding Arguments of Verse and Prose?
And no green thing afore the Door, that shews,
Or speaks a Wedding?

SCRIBEN - Those were Verses now,
Your Worship spake, and run upon vive veet.

TURFE - Feet, vrom my Mouth, D'oge? Leave your,
'zurd uppinions:
And get me in some Boughs.

SCRIBEN - Let 'em ha' Leaves first.
There's nothing green but Bays and Rosemary.

PUPPY - And they're too good for strewings, your Maids say.

TURFE - You take up 'Dority still, to vouch against me.
All the twelve Smocks i' the house, zur, are your Authors.
Get some fresh Hay then, to lay under foot:
Some Holly and Ivy, to make vine the Posts:

Is't not Son Valentine's day? and Mrs. Awdrey,
Your young Dame to be married? I wonder Clay
Should be so tedious: He's to play Son Valentine!
And the Clown sluggard's not come fro' Kilborn yet?

MEDLAY - Do you call your Son i' Law Clown, and't please your Worship?

TURFE - Yes, and vor worship too, my neighbour Medlay.
A Middlesex Clown, and one of Finsbury:
They were the first Colon's o' the Kingdom here:
The Primitory Colon's, my D'ogenes says.
Where's D'ogenes, my Writer, now? What were those
You told me, D'ogenes, were the first Colon's
O' the Countrey, that the Romans brought in here?

SCRIBEN - The Colony. Sir, Colonus is an Inhabitant:
A Clown Original: as you'ld zay a Farmer, a Tiller o' th' Earth,
E're sin' the Romans planted their Colony first,
Which was in Meddlesex.

TURFE - Why so? I thank you heartily, good D'ogenes, you ha' zertified me.
I had rather be an ancient Colon, (as they zay) a Clown of Middlesex:
A good rich Farmer, or High Constable.
I'ld play hun 'gain a Knight, or a good Squire;
Or Gentleman of any other County
I' the Kingdom.

TO-PAN - Out-cept Kent, for there they landed
All Gentlemen, and came in with the Conquerour,
Mad Julius Cæsar, who built Dover-Castle:
My Ancestor To-Pan, beat the first Kettle-Drum
Avore 'hun, here vrom Dover on the March:
Which piece of Monumental Copper hangs
Up, scour'd, at Hammer-smith yet; for there they came
Over the Thames, at a low Water-mark;
Vore either London, I, or Kingston-Bridge—
I doubt were kursin'd.

TURFE - Zee, who is here: John Clay!
Zon Valentine, and Bridegroom! ha' you zeen
Your Valentine-Bride yet, sin' you came? John Clay?

ACT I. SCENE IV

[To them.
CLAY.

CLAY - No wusse. Che lighted, I, but now i' the yard:
Puppy ha' scarce unswadled my legs yet.

TURFE - What? wispes o' your Wedding-day, zon?
This is right
Originous Clay: and Clay o' Kilborn too!
I would ha' had Boots o' this day, zure, zon.

CLAY - I did it to save charges: we mun dance,
O' this day, zure: and who can dance in boots?
No, I got on my best straw-coloured stockins,
And swaddel'd 'em over to zave Charges; I.

TURFE - And his new Shamois Doublet too with Points:
I like that yet: and his long Sawsedge-hose,
Like the Commander of Four smoaking Tile-kills,
Which he is Captain of: Captain of Kilborn:
Clay with his Hat turn'd up o' the leer side too:
As if he would leap my Daughter yet e'er night,
And spring a new Turfe to the old House.
Look, and the Wenches ha' not vound 'un out,
And do parzent un with a Van of Rosemary,
And Bays, to vill a Bow-pot, trim the Head
Of my best Vore-horse; we shall all ha' Bride-laces,
Or Points, I zee; my Daughter will be valiant,
And prove a very Mary Anbry i' the business.

CLENCH - They zaid your Worship had sur'd her to Squire Tub
Of Totten-Court here; all the Hundred rings on't.

TURFE - A Tale of a Tub, Sir, a meer Tale of 'a' Tub.
Lend it no Ear I pray you: The Squire Tub
Is a fine Man, but he is too fine a Man,
And has a Lady Tub too to his Mother:
I'll deal with none o' those vine silken Tubs.
John Clay, and Cloth-breech for my Money and Daughter.
Here comes another old Boy too, vor his Colours

[Enter FATHER ROSIN.

Will stroak down my Wives Udder of Purses, empty
Of all her Milk-money, this Winter Quarter:
Old Father Rosin, the chief Minstrel here:
Chief Minstrel too of Highgate: she has hir'd him
And all, his two Boys for a day and a half,
And now they come for Ribbanding, and Rosemary:
Give 'em enough Girls, gi' 'em enough, and take it
Out in his Tunes anon.

CLENCH - I'll ha' Tom Tiler,
For our John Clay's sake, and the Tile-kills, zure.

MEDLAY - And I the jolly Joyner, for mine own sake.

TO-PAN - I'll ha'the joviall Tinker for To-Pan's sake.

TURFE - We'll all be jovy this day, vor son Valentine.
My sweet son John's sake.

SCRIBEN - There's another reading now:
My Mr. reads it Son, and not Sin Valentine.

PUPPY - Nor Zim: And he is i'the right. He is high Constable.
And who should read above 'un, or avor 'hun?

TURFE - Son John shall bid us welcome all, this day:
We'll zerve under his colours: Lead the troop John,
And Puppy, see the Bells ring. Press all noises
Of Finsbury, in our name; D'ogenes Scriben
Shall draw a score of warrants vor the business.
Do's any wight perzent hir Majesties person,
This Hundred, 'bove the high Constable?

ALL - No, no.

TURFE - Use our Authority then, to the utmost on't.

ACT I. SCENE V

SIR HUGH, PREAMBLE, METAPHOR.

SIR HUGH - So, you are sure, Sir, to prevent 'hem all;
And throw a block i' the Bride-grooms way,
John Clay,
That he will hardly leap o'er.

PREAMBLE - I conceive you,
Sir Hugh; as if your Rhetorick would say,
Whereas the Father of her is a Turfe,
A very superficies of the earth;
He aims no higher, then to match in clay;
And there hath pitch'd his rest.

SIR HUGH - Right Justice Bramble?
You ha' the winding wit, compassing all.

PREAMBLE - Subtile Sir Hugh, you now are i' the wrong,
And err with the whole Neighbour-hood, I must tell you;
For you mistake my name. Justice Preamble
I write my self; which with the ignorant Clowns here,
(Because of my Profession of the Law,
And place o' the peace) is taken to be Bramble.

But all my warrants, Sir, do run Preamble: Richard Preamble.

SIR HUGH - Sir I thank you for't.
That your good worship, would not let me run
Longer in error, but would take me up thus —

PREAMBLE - You are my learned, and canonick neighbour:
I would not have you stray; but the incorrigible
Knot-headed beast, the Clowns, or Constables,
Still let them graze; eat Salads; chew the Cud:
All the town-musick will not move a log.

SIR HUGH - The Beetle and wedges will where you will have 'hem.

PREAMBLE - True, true, Sir Hugh, here comes Miles Metaphor,
My Clerk: He is the man shall carry it, Canon,
By my instructions.

SIR HUGH - He will do't ad unguem:
Miles Metaphore: He is a pretty fellow.

PREAMBLE - I love not to keep shadowes, or half-wits,
To foil a business. Metaphore! you ha' seen
A King ride fort hin'forth in' state.

METAPHOR - Sir, that I have:
King Edward our late Leige, and soveraign Lord:
And have set down the pomp.

PREAMBLE - Therefore I ask'd you,
Ha' you observ'd the Messengers o' the Chamber;
What habits they were in?

METAPHOR - Yes, Minor Coats.
Unto the guard, a Dragon, and a grey-hound,
For the supporters of the Arms.

PREAMBLE - Well mark'd;
You know not any of 'em?

METAPHOR - Here's one dwells
In Maribone.

PREAMBLE - Ha' you acquaintance with him,
To borrow his coat an hour?

SIR HUGH - Or but his badge,
'Twill serve: A little thing he wears on his breast.

PREAMBLE - His coat, I say, is of more authority:
Borrow his coat for an hour. I do love

To do all things compleatly, Canon Hugh;
Borrow his coat, Miles Metaphor, or nothing.

METAPHOR - The Taberd of his office, I will call it,
Or the Coat-armour of his place: and so
Insinuate with him by that Trope—.

PREAMBLE - I know your powers of Rhetorick, Metaphor.
Fetch him off in a fine figure for his coat I say.

[METAPHOR goes out.

SIR HUGH - I'll take my leave, Sir, of your worship too:
Because I may expect the issue anon.

PREAMBLE - Stay, my diviner Counsel, take your fee;
We that take fees, allow' hem to our Counsel;
And our prime learned Counsel, double fees:
There are a brace of Angels to support you
I' your Foot-walk this Frost, for fear of falling,
Or spraying of a point of Matrimony,
When you come at it.

SIR HUGH - I' your Worships service:
That the Exploit is done, and you possest
Of Mrs. Awdrey Turfe.

PREAMBLE - I like your Project.

[PREAMBLE goes out.

SIR HUGH - And I, of this effect of two to one;
It worketh i' my Pocket, 'gainst the Squire,
And his half bottom here, of half a Piece:
Which was not worth the stepping o'er the Stile for:
His Mother has quite ma rr'dmarr'd him: Lady Tub,
She's such a Vessel of Fæces: all dry'd Earth!
Terra damnata! not a drop of Salt!
Or Petre in her! All her Nitre is gone.

ACT I. SCENE VI

LADY TUB, POL-MARTIN.

LADY TUB – Is the Nag ready Martin? call the Squire.
This frosty morning we will take the Air,
About the Fields: for I do mean to be
Some-bodies Valentine, i' my Velvet Gown,
This morning, though it be but a Beggarman.

Why stand you still, and do not call my Son?

POL-MARTIN - Madam, if he had couched with the Lamb,
He had no doubt been stirring with the Lark:
But he sat up at Play, and watch'd the Cock,
Till his first warning chid him off to rest.
Late Watchers are no early Wakers, Madam:
But if your Ladiship will have him call'd.

LADY TUB - Will have him call'd? Wherefore did I, Sir, bid him
Be call'd, you Weazel, Vermine of an Huisher?
You will return your Wit to your first stile
Of Marten Polcat, by these stinking Tricks,
If you do use 'em: I shall no more call you
Pol-martin, by the Title of a Gentleman,
If you go on thus—

POL-MARTIN - I am gone.

[Goes out.

LADY TUB - Be quick then,
I' your come off: and make amends you Stote!
Was ever such a Full-mart for an Huisher,
To a great worshipful Lady, as my self;
Who, when I heard his Name first, Martin Polcat,
A stinking Name, and not to be pronounc'd
Without a Reverence.

In any Ladies presence: my very heart e'en earn'd, seeing the Fellow
Young, pretty and handsome; being then, I say,
A Basket-Carrier, and a man condemn'd
To the Salt-peter Works; made it my Suit
To Mr. Peter Tub, that I might change it;
And call him as I do now, by Pol-martin,
To have it sound like a Gentleman in an Office,
And made him mine own Fore-man, daily Waiter,
And he to serve me thus! Ingratitude!
Beyond the Courseness yet of any Clownage,

[He returns.

Shew'n to a Lady! what now, is he stirring?

POL-MARTIN - Stirring betimes out of his Bed, and ready.

LADY TUB - And comes he then?

POL-MARTIN - No, Madam, he is gone.

LADY TUB - Gone? whither? ask the Porter: Where's he gone?

POL-MARTIN - I met the Porter, and have ask'd him for him;
He says, he let him forth an hour a-go.

LADY TUB - An hour ago! what business could he have
So early? Where is his Man, grave Basket Hilts?
His Guide and Governour?

POL-MARTIN - Gone with his Master.

LADY TUB - Is he gone too? O that same surly Knave,
Is his right hand; and leads my Son amiss.
He has carried him to some drinking Match, or other:
Pol-martin, I will call you so again:
I' am Friends with you now. Go, get your Horse, and ride
To all the Towns about here, where his haunts are;
And cross the Fields to meet, and bring me word:
He cannot be gone far, being a foot.
Be curious to inquire him: and bid Wispe,
My Woman, come, and wait on me. The love
We Mothers bear our Sons, we ha' bought with pain,
Makes us oft view them, with too careful Eyes,
And over-look 'em with a jealous fear,
Out-fitting Mothers.

ACT I. SCENE VII

LADY TUB, WISPE.

LADY TUB - How now, Wispe? Ha' you
A Valentine yet? I'm taking th' air to chuse one.

WISPE - Fate send your Ladyship a fit one then.

LADY TUB - What kind of one is that?

WISPE - A proper Man,
To please your Ladyship.

LADY TUB - Out o' that Vanity,
That takes the foolish Eye: Any poor creature,
Whose want may need my alms, or courtesie,
I rather wish; so Bishop Valentine
Left us Example to do Deeds of Charity;
To feed the hungry, cloath the naked, visit
The weak and sick; to entertain the poor,
And give the dead a Christian Funeral:
These were the works of Piety he did practise,
And bade us imitate; not look for Lovers,

Or handsome Images to please our Senses.
I pray thee, Wispe, deal freely with me now:
We are alone, and may be merry a little:
Tho' art none o' the Court-Glories, nor the Wonders
For Wit or Beauty i' the City: tell me,
What Man would satisfie thy present Fancy?
Had thy ambition leave to chuse a Valentine,
Within the Queens Dominion, so a Subject.

WISPE - Yo' ha' gi' me a large scope, Madam, I confess,
And I will deal with your Ladyship sincerely:
I'll utter my whole heart to you. I would have him
The bravest, richest, and the properest Man
A Taylor could make up; or all the Poets,
With the Perfumers: I would have him such,
As not another Woman, but should spite me:
Three City-Ladies should run mad for him:
And Country-Madams infinite.

LADY TUB - You'ld spare me,
And let me hold my Wits?
Wis. I should with you—
For the young Squire, my Master's sake, dispense
A little; but it should be very little.
Then all the Court-Wives I'ld ha' jealous of me,
As all their Husbands jealous of them:
And not a Lawyers Puss of any Quality,
But lick her lips, for a snatch in the Terme time.

LADY TUB - Come,
Let's walk: we'll hear the rest as we go on:
You are this Morning in a good Vein, Dido:
Would I could be as merry. My Son's absence
Troubles me not a little: though I seek
These ways to put it off; which will not help:
Care that is entred once into the Breast,
Will have the whole possession, ere it rest.

ACT II. SCENE I

TURFE, CLAY, MEDLAY, CLENCH, TO-PAN, SCRIBEN, PUPPY.

TURFE - Zon Clay, cheer up, the better leg avore:
This is a veat is once done, and no more.

CLENCH - And then 'tis done vor ever, as they say.

MEDLAY - Right! vor a Man ha' his hour, and a Dog his day.

TURFE - True, Neighbour Medlay, yo' are still In-and-In.

MEDLAY - I would be Mr. Constable, if ch' could win.

TO-PAN - I zay, John Clay, keep still on his old gate:
Wedding and hanging both go at a rate.

TURFE - Well said, To-Pan: you ha' still the hap to hit
The Nail o' the head at a close: I think there never
Marriage was manag'd with a more avisement,
Than was this Marriage, though I say't, that should not;
Especially 'gain' mine own Flesh and Blood,
My wedded Wife. Indeed my Wife would ha' had
All the young Batchelors and Maids, forsooth,
O' the zix Parishes hereabout: But I
Cry'd none, sweet Sybil: none of that gear, I:
It would lick zalt, I told her, by her leave.
No, three or vour our wise, choice honest neighbours:
Upstantial persons: Men that ha' born Office:
And mine own Family would be enough
To eat our Dinner. What? Dear Meat's a Thief:
I know it by the Butchers, and the Market-volk;
Hum drum I cry. No half-Ox in a Pye:
A man that's bid to Bride-Ale, if he ha' Cake,
And Drink enough, he need not vear his stake.

CLENCH - 'Tis right: he has spoke as true as a Gun: believe it.

TURFE - Come, Sybil, come: Did not I tell you o' this?
This Pride, and muster of women would mar all?
Six women to one Daughter and a Mother!
The Queen (God save her) ha' no more her self.

DAME TURFE - Why, if you keep so many, Mr. Turfe,
Why should not all present our Service to her?

TURFE - Your Service? Good! I think you'll write to her shortly,
Your very loving and obedient Mother.

Come, send your Maids off, I will have 'em sent
Home again, Wife: I love no Trains o' Kent,
Or Christendom, as they say.

SCRIBEN - We will not back,
And leave our Dame.

MEDLAY - Why should her Worship lack
Her Tale of Maids, more than you do of Men?

TURFE - What, mutining, Madge?

TO-PAN - Zend back your
C'lons agen.
And we will vollow.

ALL - Else we'll guard our Dame.

TURFE - I ha' zet the Nest of Wasps all on a flame.

DAME TURFE - Come, you are such another, Mr. Turfe:
A Clod you should be call'd, of a High Constable:
To let no Musick go afore your Child
To Church, to chear her Heart up this cold Morning.

TURFE - You are for Father Rosin, and his Consort
Of fidling Boys, the great Feates, and the less:
Because you have entertain'd 'em all from Highgate.
To shew your Pomp, you'ld ha' your Daughter and Maids
Dance o'er the Fields like Fairies, to Church, this Frost?
I'll ha' no Rondels, I, i' the Queens Paths;
Let 'un scrape the Gut at home, where they ha' fill'd it
At After-noon.

DAME TURFE - I'll ha' 'em play at Dinner.
She is i' th' right, Sir; vor your Wedding-Dinner
Is starv'd without the Musick.

MEDLAY - If the Pies
Come not in piping hot, you ha' lost that Proverb.

TURFE - I yield to truth: Wife, are you sussified?

TO-PAN - A right good Man! when he knows right, he loves it.

SCRIBEN - And he will know't, and shew't too by his place
Of being High Constable, if no where else.

ACT II. SCENE II

[To them.
HILTS bearded, booted and spurr'd.

HILTS - Well over-taken, Gentlemen! I pray you,
Which is the Queens High Constable among you?

PUPPY - The tallest Man: who should be else, do you think?

HILTS - It is no matter what I think, young Clown:
Your answer savours of the Cart.

PUPPY - How? Cart?
And Clown? Do you know whose Team you speak to?
Hi. No: nor I care not: Whose Jade may you be?

PUPPY - Jade? Cart? and Clown? O for a lash of
Whip-cord!
Three-knotted Cord!

HILTS - Do you mutter? Sir, snorle this way,
That I may hear, and answer what you say,
With my School-dagger, 'bout your Costard, Sir.
Look to't, young Growse: I'll lay it on, and sure;
Take't off who's wull.

CLENCH - Nay, 'pray you Gentleman—

HILTS - Go to: I will not bate him an ace on't.
What? Rowle-powle? Maple-face? All Fellows?

PUPPY - Do you hear, Friend? I would wish you vor your good,
Tie up your brended Bitch there, your Dun rusty
Pannier-hilt Poinard: and not vex the Youth
With shewing the Teeth of it. We now are going
To Church, in way of Matrimony, some on us.
Th'a'rung all in a' ready. If it had not,
All the Horn-Beasts are grazing i' this Close,
Should not ha' pull'd me hence, till this Ash-plant
Had rung Noon o' your Pate, Mr. Broom-beard.

HILTS - That would I fain zee, quoth the blind George
Of Holloway: Come, Sir.

AWDREY - O their naked weapons!

TO-PAN - For the Passion of Man, hold Gentleman, and Puppy.

CLAY - Murder, O Murder!

AWDREY - O my Father and Mother!

DAME TURFE - Husband, what do you mean? Son Clay, for
God's sake—

TURFE - I charge you in the Queens Name, keep the peace.

HILTS - Tell me o' no Queen, or Keysar: I must have
A Leg, or a Hanch of him, e're I go.

MEDLAY - But, Zir,
You must obey the Queens High Officers.

HILTS - Why must I, Goodman Must?

MEDLAY - You must, an' your wull.

TURFE - Gentleman, I'm here for Fault, High Constable—

HILTS - Are you zo? what then?

TURFE - I pray you, Sir, put up
Your Weapons; do, at my Request: For him,
On my Authority, he shall lie by the heels,
Verbatim continente, an' I live.

DAME TURFE - Out on him for a Knave: what a dead fright
He has put me into: Come, Awdrey, do not shake.

AWDREY - But is not Puppy hurt? nor the t' other man?

CLAY - No Bun; but had not I cry'd Murder, I wuss —

PUPPY - Sweet Goodman Clench, I pray you revise my Master,
I may not zit i' the Stocks, till the Wedding be past,
Dame, Mrs. Awdrey: I shall break the Bride-Cake else.

CLENCH - Zomething must be to save Authority, Puppy.

DAME TURFE - Husband—

CLENCH - And Gossip—

AWDREY - Father—

TURFE - 'Treat me not.
It is i' vain. If he lie not by the heels,
I'll lie there for 'un. I'll teach the Hine,
To carry a Tongue in his Head to his Superiours.

HILTS - This 's a wise Constable! where keeps he School?

CLENCH - In Kentish-Town; a very survere man.

HILTS - But as survere as he is, let me, Sir, tell him,
He sha' not lay his Man by the heels for this.
This was my Quarrel: And by his Office leave,
If't carry 'un for this, it shall carry double;
Vor he shall carry me too.

TURFE - Breath of Man!
He is my Chattel, mine own hired Goods:
An' if you do abet 'un in this matter,
I'll clap you both by the heels, ankle to ankle.

HILTS - You'll clap a Dog of Wax as soon, old Blurt?
Come, spare not me, Sir; I am no Man's Wife:
I care not, I, Sir, not three skips of a Louse for you,
And you were Ten tall Constables, not I.

TURFE - Nay, pray you, Sir, be not angry; but content:
My Man shall make you what amends you'll ask 'un.

HILTS - Let 'hun mend his Manners then, and know his
Betters: It's all I ask 'un: and 'twill be his own,
And's Master's too, another day. Che vore 'hun.

MEDLAY - As right as a Club still. Zure this angry man
Speaks very near the mark, when he is pleas'd.

PUPPY - I thank you, Sir; an' I meet you at Kentish-Town,
I ha' the Courtesie o' Hundred for you.

HILTS - Gramercy, good High Constables Hine. But hear you?
Mass Constable, I have other manner o' matter,
To bring you about, than this. And so it is,
I do belong to one o' the Queens Captains;
A Gent'man o' the Field, one Captain Thum's,
I know not whether you know 'un, or no: It may be
You do, and't may be you do not again.

TURFE - No, I assure you on my Constable-ship,
I do not know 'un.

HILTS - Nor I neither, i' faith.
It skills not much; my Captain, and my self,
Having occasion to come riding by, here,
This morning, at the corner of Saint John's Wood,
Some mile o' this Town, were set upon
By a sort of Countrey Fellows; that not only
Beat us, but robb'd us most sufficiently;
And bound us to our behaviour, hand and foot;
And so they left us. Now, Don Constable,
I am to charge you in her Majesties Name,
As you will answer it at your apperil,
That forthwith you raise Hue and Cry i' the Hundred,
For all such persons as you can despect,
By the length and breadth o' your Office: vor I tell you,
The loss is of some value; therefore look to't.

TURFE - As Fortune mend me, now, or any Office
Of a thousand pound, if I know what to zay,
Would I were dead; or vaire hang'd up at Tiburn,
If I do know what course to take; or how
To turn my self; just at this time too, now,

My Daughter is to be married: I'll but go
To Pancridge-Church, hard by, and return instantly,
And all my Neighbourhood shall go about it.

HILTS - Tut, Pancridge, me no Pancridge; if you let it
Slip, you will answer it, and your Cap be of Wool;
Therefore take heed, you'll feel the smart else, Constable.

TURFE - Nay, good Sir, stay. Neighbours! what think you o' this?

DAME TURFE - Faith, Man—
Odd, precious Woman, hold your tongue,
And mind your Pigs o' the Spit at home; you must
Have Ore in every thing. Pray you, Sir, what kind
Of fellows were they?
HILTS - Thieve's kind, I ha' told you.

TURFE - I mean, what kind of Men?

HILTS - Men of our make.

TURFE - Nay, but with patience, Sir; we that are Officers
Must 'quire the special marks, and all the tokens
Of the despected parties; or perhaps else
Be ne'er the near of our purpose in 'prehending 'em.
Can you tell, what 'parrel any of them wore?

HILTS - Troth no: there were so many o' un, all like
So one another: Now I remember me,
There was one busie Fellow was their Leader;
A blunt squat swad, but lower than your self,
He' had on a Leather Doublet, with long points,
And a pair of pinn'd-up breeches, like Pudding bags:
With yellow stockings, and his Hat turn'd up
With a Silver Claspe on his leer side.

DAME TURFE - By these
Marks it should be John Clay, now bless the man!

TURFE - Peace, and be nought: I think the Woman be phrensick.

HILTS - John Clay? what's he, good Mistris?

AWDREY - He that shall be
My Husband—

HILTS - How! your Husband, pretty one?

AWDREY - Yes, I shall anon be married: That's he.

TURFE - Passion o' me, undone!

PUPPY - Bless Master's Son!

HILTS - O you are well 'prehended: know you me, Sir?
Clay. No's my Record: I never zaw you avore.

HILTS - You did not? where were your Eyes then? Out at washing?

TURFE - What should a man zay? who should he trust
In these days? Hark you, John Clay, if you have
Done any such thing, tell troth, and shame the Devil.

CLENCH - Vaith do: my Gossip Turfe zays well to you, John.

MEDLAY - Speak, man, but do not convess, nor be avraid.

TO-PAN - A man is a man, and a beast's a beast, look to't.

DAME TURFE - I' the name of men or beasts! what do you do?
Hare the poor fellow out on his five Wits,
And seven Senses? Do not weep, John Clay.
I swear the poor wretch is as guilty from it,
As the Child was, was born this very morning.

CLAY - No, as I am a kyrsin Soul, would I were hang'd,
If ever I — alas, I! would I were out
Of my life, so I would I were, and in again —

PUPPY - Nay, Mrs. Awdrey will say nay to that.
No, In-and-out? an' you were out o' your life,
How should she do for a Husband? who should fall
Aboard o' her then, Ball? He's a Puppy?
No; Hannibal has no breeding: well! I say little;
But hitherto all goes well, pray it prove no better.

AWDREY - Come, Father; I would we were married: I am a cold.

HILTS - Well, Mr. Constable, this your fine Groom here,
Bridegroom, or what Groom else, soe'er he be,
I charge him with the Felony; and charge you
To carry him back forthwith to Paddington,
Unto my Captain, who stays my return there:
I am to go to the next Justice of Peace,
To get a Warrant to raise Hue and Cry,
And bring him and his Fellows all afore 'un.
Fare you well, Sir, and look to 'un, I charge you,
As yo'll answer it. Take heed, the business,
If you defer, may prejudicial you
More than you think for; zay I told you so.

[HILTS goes out.

TURFE - Here's a Bride-ale indeed? Ah zon John, zon Clay!
I little thought you would ha' prov'd a piece
Of such false Metal.

CLAY - Father, will you believe me?
Would I might never stir i' my new shooes,
If ever I would do so voul a Fact.

TURFE - Well, Neighbours, I do charge you to assist me
With 'un to Paddington. Be he a true man, so:
The better for 'un. I will do mine Office,
An' he were my own begotten a thousand times.

DAME TURFE - Why, do you hear man? Husband? Mr. Turfe?
What shall my Daughter do? Puppy, stay here.
[She follows her Husband and Neighbour's.

AWDREY - Mother, I'll go with you, and with my Father.

ACT II. SCENE III

PUPPY, AWDREY, HILTS.

PUPPY - Nay, stay, sweet Mrs. Awdrey: here are none
But one Friend (as they zay) desires to speak
A word or two, cold with you: How do you veel
Your self this frosty morning?

AWDREY - What ha' you
To do to ask, I pray you? I am a cold.

PUPPY - It seems you are hot, good Mrs. Awdrey.

AWDREY - You lye; I am as cold as Ice is: Feel else.

PUPPY - Nay, you ha' cool'd my Courage: I am past it,
I ha' done feeling with you.

AWDREY - Done with me?
I do defie you. So I do, to say
You ha' done with me: you are a sawcy Puppy.

PUPPY - O you mistake! I meant not as you mean.

AWDREY - Meant you not Knavery?   Puppy. No, not I.
Clay meant you all the Knavery, it seems,
Who rather than he would be married to you,
Chose to be wedded to the Gallows first.

AWDREY - I thought he was a dissembler; he would prove
A slippery Merchant i' the Frost. He might
Have married one first, and have been hang'd after,
If he had had a mind to't. But you men,
Fie on you.

PUPPY - Mrs. Awdrey, can you vind
I' your heart to fancy Puppy? me poor Ball?

AWDREY - You are dispos'd to jeer one, Mr. Hannibal.

[Enter HILTS.

Pity o' me! the angry man with the beard!

HILTS - Put on thy Hat, I look for no despect.
Where's thy Master?   PUPPY - Marry, he is gone
With the Picture of Despair, to Paddington.

HILTS - Pr'y thee run after 'un, and tell 'un he shall
Find out my Captain lodg'd at the Red Lyon
In Paddington; that's the Inn. Let 'un ask
Vor Captain Thum's; And take that for thy pains:
He may seek long enough else. Hie thee again.
PUPPY - Yes, Sir, you'll look to Mrs. Bride the while?

HILTS - That I will: prethee haste.

AWDREY - What, Puppy? Puppy?

HILTS - Sweet Mrs. Bride, he'll come again presently.
Here was no subtle device to get a Wench.
This Chanon has a brave pate of his own!
A shaven pate! and a right monger, y' vaith!
This was his plot! I follow Captain Thum's?
We robb'd in Saint John's Wood? I' my t'other Hose!
I laugh to think what a fine Fool's finger they have
O' this wise Constable, in pricking out
This Captain Thum's to his Neighbours: you shall see
The Tile-man too set fire on his own Kill,
And leap into it, to save himself from hanging.
You talk of a Bride-ale, here was a Bride-ale broke
I' the nick. Well: I must yet dispatch this Bride,
To mine own master, the young Squire, and then
My task is done. Gen'woman! I have in sort
Done you some wrong, but now I'll do you what right
I can: It's true, you are a proper Woman;
But to be cast away on such a Clown-pipe
As Clay; me thinks your Friends are not so wise
As Nature might have made 'em; Well, go too:

There's be tterbetter Fortune coming toward you,
An' you do not deject it. Take a vool's
Counsel, and do not stand i' your own light.
It may prove better than you think for: Look you.

AWDREY - Alas, Sir, what is't you would ha' me do?
I'ld fain do all for the best, if I knew how.

HILTS - Forsake not a good turn when 'tis offered you;
Fair Mistris Awdrey, that's your Name, I take it.

AWDREY - No Mistris, Sir, my Name is Awdrey.

HILTS - Well, so it is, there is a bold young Squire,
The Blood of Totten, Tub, and Tripoly —

AWDREY - Squire Tub, you mean? I know him: he knows me too.

HILTS - He is in love with you: and more, he's mad for you.

AWDREY - I, so he told me: in his Wits, I think.
But he's too fine for me; and has a Lady
Tub to his Mother. Here he comes himself!

ACT II. SCENE IV

TUB, HILTS, AWDREY.

TUB – O you are a trusty Governour!

HILTS - What ails you?
You do not know when yo' are well, I think:
You'ld ha' the Calf with the white Face, Sir, would you?
I have her for you here; what would you more?

TUB - Quietness, Hilts, and hear no more of it.

HILTS - No more of it, quoth you? I do not care,
If some on us had not heard so much of't,
I tell you true; A man must carry and vetch,
Like Bungy's Dog for you.

TUB - What's he?

HILTS - A Spaniel.
And scarce be spit i' the mouth for't. A good Dog
Deserves, Sir, a good bone, of a free Master:
But, an' your turns be serv'd, the Devil a bit
You care for a man after, e're a Lard of you.

Like will to like, y-faith, quoth the scabb'd Squire
To th' mangy Knight, when both met in a Dish
Of butter'd Vish. One bad, there's ne'er a good;
And not a Barrel better Herring among you.

TUB - Nay, Hilts! I pray thee grow not fram-pull now.
Turn not the bad Cow after thy good Soap.
Our plot hath hitherto tane good effect:
And should it now be troubled, or stopp'd up,
'Twould prove the utter ruine of my hopes.
I pray thee haste to Pancridge, to the Chanon:
And gi' him notice of our good success;
Will him that all things be in readiness.
Fair Awdrey, and my self, will cross the Fields,
The nearest path. Good Hilts, make thou some haste,
And meet us on the way. Come, gentle Awdrey.

HILTS - Vaith, would I had a few more geances on't:
An' you say the word, send me to Jericho.
Out-cept a man were a Post-horse, I ha' not known
The like on't; yet, an' he had kind words,
'Twould never irke 'un. But a man may break
His heart out i' these days, and get a flap
With a Fox-tail, when he has done. And there is all.

TUB - Nay, say not so Hilts: hold thee; there are Crowns—
My love bestows on thee, for thy reward,
If Gold will please thee, all my Land shall drop
In bounty thus, to recompence thy merit.

HILTS - Tut, keep your Land, and your Gold too, Sir: I
Seek neither — nother of 'un. Learn to get
More: you will know to spend that zum you have
Early enough: you are assur'd of me.
I love you too well, to live o' the spoil:
For your own sake, were there were no worse than I.
All is not Gold that glisters; I'll to Pancridge.

TUB - See how his love doth melt him into Tears!
An honest faithful Servant is a Jewel.
Now th' adventrous Squire hath time and leisure
To ask his Awdrey how she do's, and hear
A grateful answer from her. She not speaks:
Hath the proud Tyran, Frost, usurp'd the Seat
Of former Beauty in my Loves fair Cheek;
Staining the Roseate tincture of her Blood,
With the dull dye of blue congealing cold?
No, sure the weather dares not so presume
To hurt an Object of her brightness. Yet,
The more I view her, she but looks so, so.
Ha? gi' me leave to search this mystery!

O now I have it: Bride, I know your grief;
The last Nights cold hath bred in you such horror
Of the assigned Bridegroom's constitution,
The Killburn Clay-pit; that Frost-bitten marle;
That lump in Courage: melting Cake of Ice;
That the conceit thereof hath almost kill'd thee.
But I must do thee good, wench, and refresh thee.

AWDREY - You are a merry man, Squire Tub of Totten!
I have heard much o' your words, but not o' your deeds.

TUB - Thou sayest true, sweet; I' ha' been too slack in deeds.

AWDREY - Yet I was never so straight lac'd to you, Squire.

TUB - Why, did you ever love me, gentle Awdrey?

AWDREY - Love you? I cannot tell: I must hate no body,
My Father says.

TUB - Yes, Clay and Kilbourne, Awdrey,
You must hate them.

AWDREY - It shall be for your sake then.

TUB - And for my sake shall yield you that Gratuity.

[He offers to kiss her.

AWDREY - Soft and fair, Squire, there go two words to a bargain.

[She puts him back.

TUB - What are those, Awdrey?

AWDREY - Nay, I cannot tell.
My Mother zaid, zure, if you married me,
You'ld make me a Lady the first week: and put me
In, I know not what, the very day.

TUB - What was it?
Speak, gentle Awdrey, thou shalt have it yet.

AWDREY - A Velvet Dressing for my Head, it is,
They say will make one brave; I will not know
Besse Moale, nor Margery Turne-up: I will look
Another way upon 'em, and be proud.

TUB - Troth, I could wish my Wench a better Wit;
But what she wanteth there, her Face supplies.
There is a pointed lustre in her Eye

Hath shot quite through me, and hath hit my heart:
And thence it is I first receiv'd the wound,
That ranckles now, which only she can cure.
Fain would I work my self from this conceit;
But, being flesh, I cannot. I must love her,
The naked truth is: and I will go on,
Were it for nothing, but to cross my Rivals.
Come, Awdrey: I am now resolv'd to ha' thee.

ACT II. SCENE V

PREAMBLE, METAPHOR, TUB, AWDREY.

PREAMBLE - Nay, do it quickly, Miles; Why shak'st thou, Man?
Speak but his Name: I'll second thee my self.

METAPHOR - What is his Name?

PREAMBLE - Squire Tripoly, or Tub. Any thing—

METAPHOR - Squire Tub, I do arrest you
I' the Queens Majesties Name, and all the Councils.

TUB - Arrest me, Varlet?

PREAMBLE - Keep the Peace, I charge you.

TUB - Are you there, Justice Bramble? Where's your Warrant?

PREAMBLE - The Warrant is directed here to me,
From the whole Table; wherefore I would pray you
Be patient, Squire, and make good the Peace.

TUB - Well, at your pleasure, Justice. I am wrong'd:
Sirrah, what are you, have arrested me?

PREAMBLE - He is a Purs'yvant at Arms, Squire Tub.

METAPHOR - I am a Purs'yvant; see, by my Coat else.

TUB - Well, Purs'yvant, go with me: I'll give you Bail.

PREAMBLE - Sir, he may take no Bail. It is a Warrant,
In special from the Council, and commands
Your personal appearance. Sir, your Weapon
I must require: And then deliver you
A Prisoner to this Officer, Squire Tub.
I pray you to conceive of me no other,
Than as your Friend and Neighbour. Let my Person

Be sever'd from my Office in the Fact,
And I am clear. Here, Purs'yvant, receive him
Into your Hands; and use him like a Gentleman.

TUB - I thank you, Sir: But whither must I go now?

PREAMBLE - Nay, that must not be told you, till you come
Unto the place assign'd by his Instructions.
I'll be the Maidens Convoy to her Father,
For this time, Squire.

TUB - I thank you, Mr. Bramble.
I doubt, or fear, you will make her the Ballance
To weigh your Justice in. Pray ye do me right,
And lead not her, at least, out of the way.
Justice is blind, and having a blind Guide,
She may be apt to slip aside.

PREAMBLE - I'll see to her.

TUB - I see my wooing will not thrive. Arrested!
As I had set my rest up, for a Wife?
And being so fair for it, as I was—Well, Fortune,
Thou art a blind Bawd, and a Beggar too,
To cross me thus; and let my only Rival
To get her from me? That's the Spight of Spights.
But most I muse at, is, that I, being none
O' th' Court, am sent for thither by the Council.
My Heart is not so light as't was i' the morning.

ACT II. SCENE VI

HILTS, TUB, METAPHOR.

HILTS - You mean to make a Hoiden, or a Hare
O' me, t' hunt Counter thus, and make these doubles:
And you mean no such thing as you send about?
Where's your Sweet-heart now, I marle?

TUB - Oh, Hilts!

HILTS - I know you of old! ne'er halt afore a Criple.
Will you have a Cawdle? where's your Grief, Sir? Speak?

METAPHOR - Do you hear, Friend? Do you serve this Gentleman?

HILTS - How then, Sir? what if I do? Peradventure yea:
Peradventure nay; what's that to you, Sir? Say?

METAPHOR - Nay, pray you, Sir, I meant no harm in truth:
But this good Gentleman is arrested.

HILTS - How?
Say me that again.

TUB - Nay, Basket, never storm;
I am arrested here, upon command
From the Queens Council; and I must obey.

METAPHOR - You say, Sir, very true, you must obey.
An honest Gentleman, in faith!

HILTS - He must?

TUB - But that which most tormenteth me, is this,
That Justice Bramble hath got hence, my Awdrey.

HILTS - How? how? stand by a little, Sirrah, you,
With the Badge o' your Breast. Let's know, Sir, what you are?

METAPHOR - I am, Sir, (pray you do not look so terribly)
A Purs'yvant.

HILTS - A Purs'yvant? Your Name, Sir?

METAPHOR - My Name, Sir—

HILTS - What is't? speak?

METAPHOR - Miles Metaphor;
And Justice Preamble's Clerk.

TUB - What says he?

HILTS - Pray you,
Let us alone. You are a Purs'yvant?

METAPHOR - No, faith, Sir, would I might never stir from you,
I' is made a Purs'yvant against my Will.

HILTS - Ha! and who made you one? tell true, or my Will
Shall make you nothing instantly.

METAPHOR - Put up
Your frightful Blade; and your dead-doing look,
And I shall tell you all.

HILTS - Speak then the truth,
And the whole truth, and nothing but the truth.

METAPHOR - My Master, Justice Bramble, hearing your Master,
The Squire Tub, was coming on this way,
With Mrs. Awdrey, the High Constable's Daughter;
Made me a Purs'yvant: and gave me Warrant
To arrest him, so that he might get the Lady,
With whom he is gone to Pancridge, to the Vicar,
Not to her Fathers. This was the Device,
Which I beseech you, do not tell my Master.

TUB - O wonderful! well Basket, let him rise:
And for my free Escape, forge some Excuse.
I'll post to Paddington, t' acquaint old Turfe,
With the whole business, and so stop the Marriage.

HILTS - Well, bless thee: I do wish thee Grace to keep
Thy Masters Secrets, better, or be hang'd.

METAPHOR - I thank you for your gentle admonition.
Pray you, let me call you God-father hereafter.
And as your God-son Metaphore, I promise,
To keep my Masters Privities, seal'd up
I' the Vallies o' my trust, lock'd close for ever,
Or let me be truss'd up at Tiburne shortly.

HILTS - Thine own Wish, save, or choak thee: Come away.

ACT III. SCENE I

TURFE, CLENCH, MEDLAY, TO-PAN, CRIBEN, CLAY.

TURFE - Passion of me, was ever man thus cross'd?
All things run Arsie-Versie; up-side down.
High Constable! Now by our Lady o'Walsingham,
I had rather be mark'd out Tom Scavinger,
And with a Shovel make clean the High-ways,
Than have this Office of a Constable,
And a High Constable! The higher charge,
It brings more trouble, more vexation with it.
Neighbours, good Neighbours, 'vize me what to do:
How we shall bear us in this Huy and Cry.
We cannot find the Captain; no such man
Lodg'd at the Lion, nor came thither hurt.
The morning we ha' spent in privy search;
And by that means the Bride-Ale is deferr'd;
The Bride, she's left alone in Puppy's charge;
The Bridegroom goes under a pair of Sureties;
And held of all as a respected person.
How should we bustle forward? Gi' some counsel,
How to bestir our stumps i' these cross ways.

CLENCH - Faith, Gossip Turfe, you have, you say, Remission,
To comprehend all such as are despected:
Now would I make another privy search
Through this Town, and then you have zearch'd Two Towns.

MEDLAY - Masters, take heed, let's not vind too many:
One's enough to stay the Hang-man's stomach.
There is John Clay, who is yvound already;
A proper man: A Tile-man by his Trade:
A man, as one would zay, moulded in Clay:
As spruce as any Neigbbour'sNeighbour's Child among you:
And he (you zee) is taken on Conspition,
And two or three (they zay) what call you 'em?
Zuch as the Justices of Coram nobis
Grant — (I forget their Names, you ha' many on 'em,
Mr. High Constable, they come to you.)
I ha' it at my tongues end—Conny-boroughs,
To bring him straight avore the Zessions house.

TURFE - O, you mean Warrens, Neighbour, do you not?

MEDLAY - I, I, thick same! you know 'un well enough.

TURFE - Too well, too well; wou'd I had never known 'em.
We good Vree-holders cannot live in quiet,
But every hour new purcepts, Hues and Crys,
Put us to Requisitions night and day:
What shud a man zay, shud we leave the zearch?
I am in danger to reburse as much
As he was robb'd on; I, and pay his hurts,
If I should vollow it, all the good cheer
That was provided for the Wedding-dinner
Is spoil'd and lost. Oh, there are two vat Pigs,
A zindging by the vier: Now by Saint Tomy,
Too good to eat, but on a Wedding-day;
And then a Goose will bid you all, Come cut me.
Zun Clay, zun Clay, (for I must call thee so)
Be of good comfort; take my Muckinder,
And dry thine Eyes. If thou beest true and honest;
And if thou find'st thy Conscience clear vrom it,
Pluck up a good heart, we'll do well enough.
If not, confess a truths name. But in faith,
I durst be sworn upon all holy Books
John Clay would ne'er commit a Robbery
On his own head.

CLAY - No: Truth is my rightful Judge:
I have kept my hands, here hence, fro' evil speaking,
Lying and slandering; and my tongue from stealing,
He do not live this day, can say, John Clay,

I ha' zeen thee, but in the way of honesty.

TO-PAN - Faith, Neighbour Medlay, I durst be his Burrough,
He would not look a true man in the vace.

CLAY - I take the Town to concord, where I dwell,
All Kilburn be my witness, if I were not
Begot in bashfulness, brought up in shamefac'dness:
Let 'un bring a Dog, but to my vace, that can
Zay, I ha' beat 'un, and without a vault:
Or but a Cat, will swear upon a Book,
I have as much as zet a vier her tail;
And I'll give him, or her a Crown for 'mends.
But to give out, and zay, I have robb'd a Captain!
Receive me at the latter day, if I
E're thought of any such matter; or could mind it—

MEDLAY - No, John, you are come of too good Personage;
I think my Gossip Clench, and Mr. Turfe,
Both think, you would ra'tempt no such voul matter.

TURFE - But how unhappily it comes to pass!
Just on the Wedding-day! I cry me mercy:
I had almost forgot the Hue and Cry:
Good Neighbour Pan, you are the Third-burrow,
And D'ogenes Scriben, you my learned Writer,
Make out a new purcept — Lord, for thy Goodness,
I had forgot my Daughter, all this while;
The idle Knave hath brought no news from her.
Here comes the sneaking Puppy; What's the news?
My heart! my heart! I fear all is not well,
Some things mishap'd, that he is come without her.

ACT III. SCENE II

[To them.
PUPPY, DAME TURFE.

PUPPY - Oh, where's my Master? my Master? my Master?

DAME TURFE - Thy Master? what would'st with thy Master, man?
There's thy Master.

TURFE - What's the matter, Puppy?

PUPPY - Oh Master! oh Dame! oh Dame? oh Master!

DAME TURFE - What say'st thou to thy Master, or thy Dame?

PUPPY - Oh. John Clay! John Clay! John Clay!

TURFE - What of John Clay?

MEDLAY - Luck grant he bring not news, he shall be hang'd.

CLENCH - The world forfend, I hope it is not so well.

CLAY - Oh Lord! oh me! what shall I do? poor John!

PUPPY - Oh John Clay! John Clay! John Clay!

CLAY - Alas,
That ever I was born! I will not stay by't,
For all the Tiles in Kilburne.

DAME TURFE - What of Clay?
Speak, Puppy; what of him?

PUPPY - He hath lost, he hath lost.

TURFE - For luck sake, speak, Puppy; what hath he lost?

PUPPY - O, Awdrey, Awdrey, Awdrey!

DAME TURFE - What of my Daughter Awdrey?

PUPPY - I tell you, Awdrey—do you understand me?
Awdrey, sweet Master! Awdrey, my dear Dame—

TURFE - Where is she? what's become of her, I pray thee?

PUPPY - Oh, the Serving-man! the Serving-man! the
Serving-man!

TURFE - What talk'st thou of the Serving-man? where's Awdrey?

PUPPY - Gone with the Serving-man, gone with the Serving-man.

DAME TURFE - Good Puppy, whither is she gone with him?

PUPPY - I cannot tell: he bad me bring you word,
The Captain lay at the Lion, and before
I came again, Awdrey was gone with the Serving-man;
I tell you, Awdrey's run away with the Serving-man.

TURFE - 'Od 'socks! my woman, what shall we do now?

DAME TURFE - Now, so you help not, man, I know not, I.

TURFE - This was your pomp of maids: I told you on't.

Six maids to vollow you, and not leave one
To wait upo' your Daughter! I zaid, Pride
Would be paid one day, her old vi'pence, wife.

MEDLAY - What of John Clay, Ball Puppy?

PUPPY - He hath lost —

MEDLAY - His life for velony?

PUPPY - No, his wife by villainy.

TURFE - Now, Villains both! oh that same Hue and Cry!
Oh Neighbours! oh that cursed Serving-man!
O maids! O wife! But John Clay, where's he?

[CLAY'S first mist.

How! fled for vear, zay ye? will he slip us now?
We that are Sureties, must require 'un out.
How shall we do to find the Serving-man?
Cocks bodikins! we must not lose John Clay:
Awdrey, my daughter Awdrey too! let us zend
To all the Towns, and zeek her; but alas,
The Hue and Cry, that must be look'd unto.

ACT III. SCENE III

[To them.
TUB.

TUB - What, in a passion, Turfe?

TURFE - I, good Squire Tub.
Were never honest Varmers thus perplext?

TUB - Turfe, I am privy to thy deep unrest:
The Ground of which springs from an idle plot,
Cast by a Suitor, to your daughter Awdrey—
And thus much, Turfe, let me advertise you;
Your daughter Awdrey, met I on the way,
With Justice Bramble in her company:
Who means to marry her at Pancridge-Church.
And there is Canon Hugh, to meet them ready:
Which to prevent, you must not trust delay;
But winged speed must cross their sly intent:
Then hie thee, Turfe, haste to forbid the Banes.

TURFE - Hath Justice Bramble got my daughter Awdrey?

A little while shall he enjoy her, zure.
But O, the Hue and Cry! that hinders me:
I must pursue that, or neglect my Journey:
I'll e'en leave all, and with the patient Ass,
The over-laden Ass, throw off my burden,
And cast mine Office; pluck in my large Ears
Betimes, lest some dis-judge 'em to be Horns:
I'll leave to beat it on the broken hoof,
And ease my pasterns. I'll no more High Constables.

TUB - I cannot chuse but smile, to see thee troubled
With such a bald, half-hatched circumstance!
The Captain was not robb'd, as is reported;
That Trick the Justice craftily deviz'd,
To break the marriage with the Tile-man, Clay.
The Hue and Cry was meerly counterfeit:
The rather may you judge it to be such,
Because the Bridegroom was describ'd to be
One of the Thieves, first in the Velony.
Which, how far 'tis from him, your selves may guess:
'Twas Justice Bramble's vetch, to get the wench.

TURFE - And is this true, Squire Tub?

TUB - Believe me, Turfe,
As I am a Squire: or less, a Gentleman.

TURFE - I take my Office back, and my Authority,
Upon your Worship's words. Neighbours, I am
High Constable again: where's my zon Clay?
He shall be zon yet, wife, your meat by leisure:
Draw back the Spits.

DAME TURFE - That's done already, Man.

TURFE - I'll break this Marriage off: and afterward,
She shall be given to her first betroth'd.
Look to the meat, wife: look well to the roast.

TUB - I'll follow him aloof, to see the event.

PUPPY - Dame, Mistriss, though I do not turn the Spit,
I hope yet the Pig's Head.

DAME TURFE - Come up, Jack-sauce:
It shall be serv'd in to you.

PUPPY - No, no Service;
But a Reward for Service.

DAME TURFE - I still took you

For an unmannerly Puppy: Will you come,
And vetch more Wood to the Vier, Mr. Ball?

PUPPY - I Wood to the Vier: I shall piss it out first:
You think to make me e'en your Ox or Ass,
Or any thing. Though I cannot right my self
On you, I'll sure revenge me on your meat.

ACT III. SCENE IV

LADY TUB, POL-MARTIN, WISPE, PUPPY.

POL-MARTIN - Madam, to Kentish-Town, we are got at length;
But by the way we cannot meet the Squire:
Not by Inquiry can we hear of him.
Here is Turfe's House, the Father of the Maid.

LADY TUB - Pol-Martin, see, the streets are strew'd with herbs,
And here hath been a Wedding, Wispe, it seems!
Pray Heaven this Bridal be not for my Son!
Good Martin, knock: knock quickly: Ask for Turfe.
My thoughts misgive me, I am in such a doubt—

POL-MARTIN - Who keeps the House here?

PUPPY - Why, the Door and Walls
Do keep the House.

POL-MARTIN - I ask then, who's within?

PUPPY - Not you that are without.

POL-MARTIN - Look forth, and speak
Into the street here. Come before my Lady.

PUPPY - Before my Lady? Lord have mercy upon me:
If I do come before her, she will see
The handsom'st Man in all the Town, pardee!
Now stand I vore her, what zaith velvet she?

LADY TUB - Sirrah, whose Man are you?

PUPPY - Madam, my Masters.

LADY TUB - And who's thy Master?

PUPPY - What you tread on, Madam.

LADY TUB - I tread on an old Turfe.

PUPPY - That Turfe's my Master.

LADY TUB - A merry fellow! what's thy Name?

PUPPY - Ball Puppy
They call me at home: abroad, Hannibal Puppy.

LADY TUB - Come hither, I must kiss thee, Valentine Puppy.
Wispe! ha' you got you a Valentine?

WISPE - None, Madam:
He's the first stranger that I saw.

LADY TUB - To me
He is so, and such. Let's share him equally.

PUPPY - Help, help, good Dame. A Rescue, and in time.
Instead of Bills, with Colstaves come; instead of Spears, with Spits;
Your slices serve for slicing Swords, to save me, and my Wits:
A Lady, and her woman here, their Huisher eke by side,
(But he stands mute) have plotted how your Puppy to divide.

ACT III. SCENE V

[To them.
DAME TURFE, MAIDS.

DAME TURFE - How now? what noise is this with you, Ball Puppy?

PUPPY - Oh Dame! and fellows o' the Kitchin! arm,
Arm, for my safety; if you love your Ball:
Here is a strange thing, call'd a Lady, a Mad-dame:
And a device of hers, yclept her Woman;
Have plotted on me, in the King's High-way,
To steal me from my self, and cut me in halfs,
To make one Valentine to serve 'em both;
This for my right-side, that my left-hand loves.

DAME TURFE - So saucy, Puppy? to use no more reverence
Unto my Lady, and her Velvet Gown?

LADY TUB - Turfe's Wife, rebuke him not: Your Man doth please me
With his conceit. Hold: there are ten old Nobles,
To make thee merrier yet, half-Valentine.

PUPPY - I thank you, right-side: could my left as much,
'Twould make me a Man of Mark: young Hannibal!

LADY TUB - Dido, shall make that good; or I will for her.
Here Dido Wispe, there's for your Hannibal:
He is your Countrey-man, as well as Valentine.
Here, Mr. Hannibal: my Ladies Bounty
For her poor Woman, Wispe.

PUPPY - Brave Carthage Queen!
And such was Dido: I will ever be
Champion to her, who Juno is to thee.

DAME TURFE - Your Ladyship is very welcome here.
Please you, good Madam, to go near the House.

LADY TUB - Turfe's Wife, I come thus far to seek thy Husband,
Having some business to impart unto him.
Is he at home?

DAME TURFE - O no, and't shall please you:
He is posted hence to Pancridge, with a witness.
Young Justice Bramble has kept level coyl
Here in our Quarters, stole away our Daughter,
And Mr. Turfe's run after, as he can,
To stop the Marriage, if it will be stopp'd.

POL-MARTIN - Madam, these tidings are not much amiss!
For if the Justice have the Maid in keep,
You need not fear the marriage of your Son.

LADY TUB - That somewhat easeth my suspicious breast.
Tell me, Turfe's Wife, when was my Son with Awdrey?
How long is't, since you saw him at your House?

PUPPY - Dame, let me take this Rump out of your Mouth.

DAME TURFE - What mean you by that, Sir?

PUPPY - Rump and Tale's all one.
But I would use a Reverence for my Lady:
I would not zay surreverence, the Tale
Out o' your Mouth, but rather take the Rump.

DAME TURFE - A well-bred Youth! and vull of Favour you are.

PUPPY - What might they zay, when I were gone, if I
Not weigh'd my words? This Puppy is a Vool!
Great Hannibal's an Ass; he had no breeding:
No Lady gay, you shall not zay,
That your Val. Puppy, was so unlucky,
In speech to fail, as t' name a Tail,
Be as be may be, 'vore a fair Lady.

LADY TUB - Leave jesting; tell us, when you saw our Son.

PUPPY - Marry, it is two hours ago.

LADY TUB - Sin' you saw him?

PUPPY - You might have seen him too, if you had look'd up.
For it shin'd as brighrbright as day.

LADY TUB - 'I' Mean my Son.

PUPPY - Your Sun, and our Sun, are they not all one?

LADY TUB - Fool, thou mistak'st; I ask'd thee, for my Son!

PUPPY - I had thought there had been no more Suns than one.
I know not what you Ladies have, or may have.

POL-MARTIN - Did'st thou ne'er hear my Lady had a Son?

PUPPY - She may have twenty; but for a Son, unless
She mean precisely, Squire Tub, her Zon,
He was here now, and brought my Master word,
That Justice Bramble had got Mrs. Awdrey.
But whither he be gone, here's none can tell.

LADY TUB - Martin, I wonder at this strange discourse:
The Fool it seems tells true; my Son, the Squire,
Was doubtless here this morning. For the match,
I'll smother what I think, and staying here,
Attend the Sequel of this strange beginning.
Turfe's Wife, my people, and I will trouble thee,
Until we hear some tidings of thy Husband.
The rather, for my party Valentine.

ACT III. SCENE VI

TURFE, AWDREY, CLENCH, MEDLAY, PAN, SCRIBEN.

TURFE - Well, I have carried it, and will triumph
Over this Justice, as becomes a Constable;
And a High Constable: next our Saint George,
Who rescued the King's Daughter, I will ride;
Above Prince Arthur.

CLENCH - Or our Shore-ditch Duke.

MEDLAY - Or Pancridge Earl.

TO-PAN - Or Bevis, or Sir Guy,
Who were High Constables both.

CLENCH - One of Southampton—

MEDLAY - The t'other of Warwick-Castle.

TURFE - You shall work it
Into a Story for me, neighbour Medlay,
Over my Chimney.

SCRIBEN - I can give you, Sir,
A Roman Story of a Petty-Constable,
That had a Daughter, that was call'd Virginia,
Like Mrs. Awdrey, and as young as she;
And how her Father bare him in the business,
'Gainst Justice Appius, a Decemvir in Rome,
And Justice of Assize.

TURFE - That, that good D'ogenes!
A Learned Man is a Chronicle!

SCRIBEN - I can tell you
A thousand, of great Pompey, Cæsar, Trajan,
All the High Constables there.

TURFE - That was their place:
They were no more.

SCRIBEN - Dictator, and High Constable,
Were both the same.

MEDLAY - High Constable was more, though!
He laid Dick Tator by the heels.

TO-PAN - Dick Toter!
H' was one o' the Waights o' the City: I ha' read o' 'un:
He was a fellow would be drunk, debauch'd—
And he did zet 'un i' the Stocks indeed:
His name Vadian, and a cunning Toter.

AWDREY - Was ever silly Maid thus posted off?
That should have had three Husbands in one day;
Yet (by bad Fortune) am possest of none?
I went to Church to have been wed to Clay;
Then Squire Tub he seiz'd me on the way,
And thought to ha' had me; but he mist his aim:
And Justice Bramble (nearest of the three)
Was well nigh married to me; when by chance,
In rush'd my Father, and broke off that dance.

TURFE - I, Girl, there's ne'er a Justice on 'em all,
Shall teach the Constable to guard his own:
Let's back to Kentish-town, and there make merry;
These news will be glad tidings to my Wife:
Thou shalt have Clay, my wench. That word shall stand.
He's found by this time, sure, or else he's drown'd:
The Wedding-dinner will be spoil'd: make haste.

AWDREY - Husbands, they say, grow thick; but thin are sown.
I care not who it be, so I have one.

TURFE - I? zay you zo? Perhaps you shall ha' none, for that.

AWDREY - Now out on me! what shall I do then?

MEDLAY - Sleep, Mistris Awdrey, dream on proper Men.

ACT III. SCENE VII

HUGH, PREAMBLE, METAPHOR.

SIR HUGH – O Bone Deus! have you seen the like?
Here was Hodge, hold thine Ear fair, whilst I strike.
Body o' me, how came this gear about?

PREAMBLE - I know not, Chanon, but it falls out cross.
Nor can I make conjecture by the Circumstance
Of these Events; it was impossible,
Being so close, and politickly carried,
To come so quickly to the Ears of Turfe.
O Priest, had but thy slow delivery
Been nimble, and thy lazy Latine Tongue,
But run the Forms o'er, with that swift dispatch,
As had been requisite, all had been well!

SIR HUGH - What should have been, that never lov'd the Frier;
But thus you see th' old Adage verified,
Multa cadunt inter—you can guess the rest.
Many things fall between the Cup and Lip:
And though they touch, you are not sure to drink.
You lack'd good fortune, we had done our parts:
Give a Man fortune, throw him i' the Sea.
The properer Man, the worse luck: Stay a time;
Tempus edax — In time the stately Ox, &c.
Good Counsels lightly never come too late.

PREAMBLE - You, Sir, will run your Counsels out of breath.

SIR HUGH - Spur a free Horse, he'll run himself to death.

Sancti Evangelistæ! Here comes Miles!

PREAMBLE - What news, man, with our new-made Purs'yvant?

METAPHOR - A Pursuyvant? would I were, or more pursie,
And had more store of money; or less pursie,
And had more store of breath: you call me Purs'yvant!
But I could never vaunt of any Purse
I had, sin' yo' were my God-fathers and God-mothers,
And ga' me that nick-name.

PREAMBLE - What now's the matter?

METAPHOR - Nay, 'tis no matter. I ha' been simply beaten.

SIR HUGH - What is become o' the Squire, and thy Prisoner?

METAPHOR - The lines of Blood, run streaming from my Head,
Can speak what Rule the Squire hath kept with me.

PREAMBLE - I pray thee, Miles, relate the manner, how?

METAPHOR - Be't known unto you, by these Presents, then,
That I, Miles Metaphor, your Worship's Clerk,
Have e'en been beaten, to an Allegory,
By multitude of hands. Had they been but
Some five or six, I had whip'd 'em all, like Tops
In Lent, and hurl'd 'em into Hoblers-hole;
Or the next Ditch: I had crack'd all their Costards,
As nimbly as a Squirrel will crack Nuts:
And flourished like to Hercules, the Porter,
Among the Pages. But, when they came on
Like Bees about a Hive, Crows about Carrion,
Flies about Sweet-meats; nay, like Water-men
About a Fare: then was poor Metaphor,
Glad to give up the Honour of the Day,
To quit his charge to them, and run away
To save his life, only to tell this news.

SIR HUGH - How indirectly all things have fall'n out!
I cannot chuse but wonder what they were,
Rescued your Rival from the keep of Miles:
But most of all I cannot well digest,
The manner how our purpose came to Turfe.

PREAMBLE - Miles, I will see that all thy Hurts be drest.
As for the Squires Escape, it matters not:
We have by this means disappointed him;
And that was all the main I aimed at.
But Chanon Hugh, now muster up thy Wits,
And call thy thoughts into the Consistory.

Search all the secret corners of thy Cap,
To find another queint devised drift,
To disappoint her Marriage with this Clay:
Do that, and I'll reward thee jovially.

SIR HUGH - Well said, Magister Justice. If I fit you not
With such a new, and well-laid Stratagem,
As never yet your Ears did hear a finer,
Call me, with Lily, Bos, Fur, Sus atq; Sacerdos.

PREAMBLE - I hear, there's comfort in thy words yet, Chanon.
I'll trust thy Regulars, and say no more.

METAPHOR - I'll follow too. And if the dapper Priest
Be but as cunning, point in his device,
As I was in my lye: My Master Preamble
Will stalk, as led by the Nose with these new Promises,
And fatted with Supposes of fine Hopes.

ACT III. SCENE VIII

TURFE, DAME TURFE, LADY TUB, POL-MARTIN, AWDREY, PUPPY.

TURFE - Well, Madam, I may thank the Squire your Son:
For, but for him, I had been over-reacht.

DAME TURFE - Now Heavens Blessing light upon his Heart:
We are beholden to him, indeed, Madam.

LADY TUB - But can you not resolve me where he is?
Nor about what his Purposes were bent?

TURFE - Madam, they no whit were concerning me:
And therefore was I less inquisitive.

LADY TUB - Fair Maid, in faith, speak truth, and not dissemble:
Do's he not often come, and visit you?

AWDREY - His Worship, now and then, please you, takes pains
To see my Father and Mother: But, for me,
I know my self too mean for his high thoughts
To stoop at, more than asking a light question,
To make him merry, or to pass his time.

LADY TUB - A Sober Maid! call for my Woman, Martin.

POL-MARTIN - The Maids, and her half-Valentine, have ply'd her
With courtsie of the Bride-Cake, and the Bowle,
As she is laid a while.

LADY TUB - O, let her rest!
We will cross o'er to Canterbury, in the interim;
And so make home. Farewel, good Turf, and thy Wife.
I wish your Daughter Joy.

TURFE - Thanks to your Ladiship:
Where is John Clay now? have you seen him yet?

DAME TURFE - No, he has hid himself out of the way,
For fear o' the Hue and Cry.

TURFE - What, walks that Shadow
Avore 'un still? Puppy, go seek 'un out,
Search all the corners that he haunts unto,
And call 'un forth. We'll once more to the Church,
And try our vortunes. Luck, Son Valentine:
Where are the Wise Men all of Finsbury?

PUPPY - Where Wise Men 'Wise Men' should be; at the Ale, and Bride-Cake.
I would this Couple had their Destiny,
Or to be hang'd, or married out o' the way:

[Enter the Neighbours to TURFE.

Man cannot get the mount'nance of an Egg-shell,
To stay his Stomach. Vaith, vor mine own part,
I have zup'd up so much Broth, as would have cover'd
A Leg o' Beef, o'er Head and Ears, i' the Porridge-Pot:
And yet I cannot sussifie wild Nature.
Would they were once dispatch'd, we might to dinner.
I am with Child of a huge Stomach, and long,
Till by some honest Midwife-piece of Beef,
I be deliver'd of it: I must go now,
And hunt out for this Kilbourn Calf, John Clay:
Whom where to find, I know not, nor which way.

ACT III. SCENE IX

[To them.
CHANON HUGH, like CAPTAIN THUMBS.

SIR HUGH - Thus as a Beggar in a King's disguise,
Or an old Cross, well sided with a May-pole,
Comes Chanon Hugh, accoutred, as you see,
Disguis'd, Soldado like: Mark his Device:
The Chanon, is that Captain Thum's, was robb'd:
These bloody Scars upon my Face, are Wounds:
This Scarff upon mine Arm, shews my late Hurts:

And thus am I to gull the Constable.
Now have among you, for a Man at Arms:
Friends, by your leave; which of you is one Turfe?

TURFE - Sir, I am Turfe, if you would speak with me.

SIR HUGH - With thee, Turfe, if thou beest High Constable.

TURFE - I am both Turfe, Sir, and High Constable.

SIR HUGH - Then, Turfe, or Scurfe, High, or Low Constable:
Know, I was once a Captain at Saint Quintins,
And passing cross the ways over the Countrey,
This Morning, betwixt this and Hamsted-heath,
Was by a Crew of Clowns robb'd, bobb'd, and hurt.
No sooner had I got my Wounds bound up,
But with much pain, I went to the next Justice,
One Mr. Bramble, here, at Maribone:
And here a Warrant is, which he hath directed
For you, one Turfe; if your Name be Toby Turfe;
Who have let fall (they say) the Hue and Cry:
And you shall answer it afore the Justice.

TURFE - Heaven and Hell, Dogs, Devils, what is this?
Neighbours, was ever Constable thus cross'd?
What shall we do?

MEDLAY - Faith, all go hang our selves:
I know no other way to scape the Law.

PUPPY - News, news, O news—

TURFE - What, hast thou found out Clay?

PUPPY - No, Sir, the news is, that I cannot find him.

SIR HUGH - Why do you dally, you damn'd Russet Coat?
You Peasant, nay, you Clown, you Constable;
See that you bring forth the suspected Party,
Or by mine Honour (which I won in Field)
I'll make you pay for it, afore the Justice.

TURFE - Fie, fie: O Wife, I'm now in a fine pickle.
He that was most suspected is not found:
And which now makes me think, he did the Deed,
He thus absents him, and dares not be seen.
Captain, my Innocence will plead for me.
Wife, I must go, needs, whom the Devil drives:
Pray for me, Wife, and Daughter; pray for me.

SIR HUGH - I'll lead the way: Thus is the Match put off:

And if my Plot succeed, as I have laid it,
My Captain-ship shall cost him many a Crown.

[They go out.

DAME TURFE - So, we have brought our Eggs to a fair Market.
Out on that Villain, Clay: Would he do a Robbery?
I'll ne'er trust smooth-fac'd Tile-man for his sake.

AWDREY - Mother, the still Sow eats up all the Draffe.

[They go out.

PUPPY - Thus is my Master, Toby Turfe, the Pattern
Of all the painful a'ventures now in Print.
I never could hope better of this match:
This Bride-Ale: For the night before to day,
(Which is within man's memory, I take it,)
At the Report of it, an Ox did speak;
Who dy'd soon after: A Cow lost her Calf:
The Bell-wether was flea'd for't: A fat Hog
Was sing'd, and wash'd, and shaven all over; to
Look ugly 'gainst this day: The Ducks they quak'd;
The Hens too cackled: at the noise whereof,
A Drake was seen to dance a headless round:
The Goose was cut i' the head, to hear it too:
Brave Chant-it-clear, his noble Heart was done;
His Comb was cut: And two or three o' his Wives,
Or fairest Concubines, had their Necks broke,
Ere they would zee this day; To mark the verven
Heart of a Beast, the very Pig, the Pig,
This very morning, as he was a roasting,
Cry'd out his Eyes, and made a show, as he would
Ha' bit in two the Spit; as he would say,
There shall no Roast-meat be this dismal day.
And zure, I think, if I had not got his Tongue
Between my Teeth, and eat it, he had spoke it.
Well, I will in, and cry too; never leave
Crying, until our Maids may drive a Buck
With my salt Tears at the next washing-day.

ACT IV. SCENE I

PREAMBLE, HUGH, TURFE, METAPHOR.

PREAMBLE - Keep out those fellows; I'll ha none come in,
But the High Constable, the Man of Peace,
And the Queens Captain, the brave Man of War.
Now, Neighbour Turfe, the Cause why you are call'd

Before me, by my Warrant, but unspecified,
Is this; and pray you mark it thoroughly!
Here is a Gentleman, and, as it seems,
Both of good Birth, fair Speech, and peaceable,
Who was this morning robb'd here in the Wood:
You, for your part, a man of good Report,
Of Credit, Landed, and of fair Demeans,
And by Authority, High Constable;
Are, notwithstanding, touch'd in this Complaint,
Of being careless in the Hue and Cry.
I cannot chuse but grieve a Soldiers loss;
And I am sorry too for your neglect,
Being my Neighbour: this is all I object.

SIR HUGH - This is not all; I can alledge far more,
And almost urge him for an Accessary.
Good Mr. Justice, gi' me leave to speak,
For I am Plaintiff. Let not Neighbourhood
Make him secure, or stand on privilege.

PREAMBLE - Sir, I dare use no partiality:
Object then what you please, so it be truth.

SIR HUGH - This more: and which is more than he can answer,
Beside his letting fall the Hue and Cry,
He doth protect the Man charg'd with the Felony,
And keeps him hid, I hear, within his House,
Because he is affied unto his Daughter.

TURFE - I do defie 'un, so shall she do too.
I pray your Worship's Favour, le' me have hearing.
I do convess, 'twas told me such a Velony,
And't not disgriev'd me a little, when 'twas told me,
Vor I was going to Church, to marry Awdrey:
And who should marry her, but this very Clay,
Who was charg'd to be the chief Thief o' 'un all.
Now I (the Halter stick me, if I tell
Your Worships any Leazins) did fore-think 'un
The truest Man, till he waz run away.
I thought I had had 'un as zure as in a Zaw-pit,
Or i' mine Oven: Nay, i' the Town-pound.
I was za sure o' 'un, I'ld ha' gi'n my life for 'un,
Till he did start. But now I zee 'un guilty,
As var as I can look at 'un. Would you ha' more?

SIR HUGH - Yes, I will have, Sir, what the Law will give me.
You gave your word to see him safe, forth-coming;
I challenge that: But that is forfeited;
Beside, your carelessness in the pursuit,
Argues your slackness, and neglect of duty,
Which ought be punish'd with severity.

PREAMBLE - He speaks but reason, Turfe. Bring forth the Man,
And you are quit: But otherwise, your word
Binds you to make amends for all his loss,
And think your self be-friended, if he take it,
Without a farther Suit, or going to Law.
Come to a Composition with him, Turfe:
The Law is costly, and will draw on charge.

TURFE - Yes, I do know, I vurst mun vee a Returney,
And then make Legs to my great Man o' Law,
To be o' my counsel, and take trouble-vees,
And yet zay nothing vor me, but devise
All district means, to ransackle me o' my money.
A Pest'lence prick the throats o' 'un. I do know 'un
As well az I was i' their Bellies, and brought up there.
What would you ha' me do? what would you ask of me?

SIR HUGH - I ask the restitution of my money;
And will not bate one penny o' the sum:
Fourscore and five pound, I ask, besides
Amendment for my hurts; my pain and suffering
Are loss enough for me, Sir, to sit down with;
I'll put it to your Worship; what you award me,
I'll take; and gi' him a general Release.

PREAMBLE - And what say you now, neighbour Turfe?

TURFE - I put it
E'en to your Worship's bitterment, hab, nab.
I shall have a chance o' the dice for't, I hope, let 'em e'en run: And—

PREAMBLE - Faith, then I'll pray you, 'cause he is my neighbour,
To take a hundred pound, and give him day.

SIR HUGH - Saint Valentine's day, I will, this very day,
Before Sun set: my Bond is forfeit else.

TURFE - Where will you ha' it paid?

SIR HUGH - Faith, I am a stranger
Here i' the Countrey: Know you Chanon Hugh,
The Vicar of Pancras?

TURFE - Yes, we who not him?

SIR HUGH - I'll make him my Attorney to receive it,
And give you a Discharge.

TURFE - Whom shall I send for't?

PREAMBLE - Why, if you please, send Metaphor, my Clerk.
And Turfe, I much commend thy willingness;
It's argument of thy integrity.

TURFE - But my Integrity shall be my zelf still:
Good Mr. Metaphor, give my Wife this Key;
And do but whisper it into her Hand:
(She knows it well enow) bid her, by that,
Deliver you the two zeal'd Bags o' Silver,
That lie i' the corner o' the Cup-board, stands
At my bed-side, they're vifty pound a piece;
And bring 'em to your Master.

METAPHOR - If I prove not
As just a Carrier as my Friend, Tom Long, was,
Then call me his Curtall, change my name of Miles,
To Guile's, Wile's, Pile's, Bile's, or the foulest name
You can devise, to cramb with, for Ale.

SIR HUGH - Come hither, Miles, bring by that token too,
Fair Awdrey; say, her Father sent for her:
Say, Clay is found, and waits at Pancras-Church,
Where I attend to marry them in haste.
For, (by this means) Miles, I may say't to thee,
Thy Master must to Awdrey married be.
But not a word but mum: go get thee gone;
Be wary of thy charge, and keep it close.

METAPHOR - O super-dainty Chanon! Vicar in cóney,
Make no delay, Miles, but away.
And bring the Wench, and Money.

SIR HUGH - Now, Sir, I see you meant but honestly;
And, but that business calls me hence away,
I would not leave you till the Sun were lower.
But, Mr. Justice, one word, Sir, with you.
By the same token, is your Mistris sent for
By Metaphore, your Clerk, as from her Father.
Who when she comes, I'll marry her to you,
Unwitting to this Turfe, who shall attend
Me at the Parsonage. This was my plot:
Which I must now make good; turn Chanon again,
In my Square Cap. I humbly take my leave.

PREAMBLE - Adieu, good Captain. Trust me, neighbour Turfe,
He seems to be a sober Gentleman:
But this distress hath somewhat stirr'd his patience.
And Men, you know, in such Extremities,
Apt not themselves to points of Courtesie;
I'm glad you ha' made this end.

TURFE - You stood my Friend:
I thank your Justice-worship; pray you be
Prezent anon, at tendring o' the Money,
And zee me have a discharge: Vor I ha' no craft
I' your Law Quiblins.

PREAMBLE - I'll secure you, neighbour.

THE SCENE INTERLOPING.

MEDLAY, CLENCH, PAN, SCRIBEN.

MEDLAY - Indeed there is a woundy luck in names, Sirs,
And a main Mystery, an' a Man knew where
To vind it. My God-sires Name, I'll tell you,
Was In-and-In Shittle, and a Weaver he was,
And it did fit his Craft: for so his Shittle
Went in, and in still; this way, and then that way.
And he nam'd me, In-and-In Medlay: which serves
A Joyners Craft, bycause that we do lay
Things in and in, in our work. But, I am truly
Architectonicus Professor, rather:
That is, (as one would zay) an Architect.

CLENCH - As I am a Varrier, and a Visicary:
Horse-Smith of Hamsted, and the whole Town Leach —

MEDLAY - Yes, you ha' done woundy Cures, Gossip Clench.

CLENCH - An' I can zee the Stale once, through a Urine-hole,
I'll give a shrewd guess, be it Man or Beast.
I cur'd an Ale-wife once, that had the Staggers
Worse than five Horses, without rowelling.
My God-phere was a Rabian, or a Jew,
(You can tell, D'oge!) They call'd 'un Doctor Rasi.

SCRIBEN - One Rasis was a great Arabick Doctor.

CLENCH - He was King Harry's Doctor, and my God-phere.

TO-PAN - Mine was a merry Greek, To-Pan, of Twyford:
A jovial Tinker, and a stopper of Holes;
Who left me Metal-man of Belsise, his Heir.

MEDLAY - But what was yours, D'oge?

SCRIBEN - Vaith, I cannot tell,
If mine were kyrsin'd, or no. But zure he had
A kyrsin Name, that he left me, Diogenes.

A mighty learned Man, but pest'lence poor.
Vor h' had no House, save an old Tub, to dwell in,
(I vind that in Records) and still he turn'd it
I' the Wind's Teeth, as't blew on his back-side,
And there they would lie rowting one at other,
A Week sometimes.

MEDLAY - Thence came A Tale of a Tub;
And the virst Tale of a Tub, old D'ogenes Tub.

SCRIBEN - That was avore Sir Peter Tub, or his Lady.

TO-PAN - I, or the Squire their Son, Tripoli Tub.

CLENCH - The Squire is a fine Gentleman!

MEDLAY - He is more:
A Gentleman and a half; almost a Knight;
Within zix Inches: That's his true measure.

CLENCH - Zure you can gage 'un.

MEDLAY - To a streak, or less:
I know his D'ameters, and Circumference:
A Knight is six Diameters; and a Squire
Is vive, and zomewhat more: I know't by compass,
And skale of Man. I have upo' my Rule here,
The just perportions of a Knight, a Squire;
With a tame Justice, or an Officer rampant,
Upo' the Bench, from the High Constable
Down to the Headborough, or Tithing-man;
Or meanest Minister o' the Peace. God save 'un.

TO-PAN - Why, you can tell us by the Squire,Square Neighbour,
Whence he is call'd a Constable, and whaffore.

MEDLAY - No, that's a Book-case: Scriben can do that.
That's writing and reading, and Records.

SCRIBEN - Two words,
Cyning and Staple, make a Constable:
As we'd say, a hold, or stay for the King.

CLENCH - All Constables are truly John's for the King,
What ere their Names are, be they Tony, or Roger.

MEDLAY - And all are sworn, as vingars o' 'the' one hand,
To hold together 'gainst the breach o' the Peace;
The High Constable is the Thumb, as one would zay,
The hold-fast o' the rest.

TO-PAN - Pray luck he speed
Well i' the business, between Captain Thums,
And him.

MEDLAY - I'll warrant 'un for a Groat;
I have his measures here in Rithmetique,
How he should bear 'un self in all the Lines
Of's Place and Office; Let's zeek 'un out.

ACT IV. SCENE II

TUB, HILTS, METAPHOR.

TUB - Hilts, how do'st thou like o' this our good days work?

HILTS - As good e'en ne'er a whit, as ne'er the better.

TUB - Shall we to Pancridge, or to Kentish-town, Hilts?

HILTS - Let Kentish-town, or Pancridge, come to us,
If either will: I will go home again.

TUB - Faith, Basket, our success hath been but bad,
And nothing prospers that we undertake;
For we can neither meet with Clay nor Awdrey,
The Chanon Hugh, nor Turfe the Constable:
We are like Men that wander in strange Woods,
And lose our selves in search of them we seek.

HILTS - This was because we rose on the wrong side;
But as I am now here, just in the mid-way,
I'll zet my Sword on the Pommel, and that line
The point valls to, we'll take: whether it be
To Kentish-town, the Church, or Home again.

TUB - Stay, stay thy Hand: here's Justice Bramble's

Enter METAPHOR.

METAPHOR - The unlucky Hare hath crost us all this day.
I'll stand aside whilst thou pump'st out of him
His Business, Hilts; and how he's now employed.

HILTS - Let me alone, I'll use him in his kind.

METAPHOR - Oh, for a Pad-horse, Pack-horse, or a Post-horse,
To bear me on his Neck, his Back, or his Crup!
I am as weary with running, as a Mill-horse
That hath led the Mill once, twice, thrice about,

After the breath hath been out of his Body.
I could get up upon a Pannier, a Pannel,
Or, to say truth, a very Pack-Saddle,
Till all my Honey were turn'd into Gall,
And I could sit in the Seat no longer:
Oh the Legs of a Lackey now, or a Foot-man,
Who is the Surbater of a Clerk currant,
And the Confounder of his tressless Dormant!
But who have we here, just in the nick?

HILTS - I am neither nick, nor in the nick: therefore
You lye, Sir Metaphor.

METAPHOR - Lye? how?

HILTS - Lye so, Sir.

[He stikes up his Heels.

METAPHOR - I lye not yet i' my throat.

HILTS - Thou ly'st o' the ground.
Do'st thou know me?

METAPHOR - Yes, I did know you too late.

HILTS - What is my Name then?

METAPHOR - Basket.

HILTS - Basket? what?

METAPHOR - Basket, the Great—

HILTS - The Great? what?

METAPHOR - Lubber—
I should say, Lover, of the Squire, his Master.

HILTS - Great is my patience, to forbear thee thus,
Thou Scrape-hill, Scoundrel, and thou skum of Man;
Uncivil, orenge-tawny-coated Clerk:
Thou cam'st but half a thing into the world,
And wast made up of patches, parings, shreds:
Thou, that when last thou wert put out of Service,
Travelled'st to Hamsted-Heath, on an Ash-we'nesday,
Where thou didst stand six weeks the Jack of Lent,
For Boys to hurle, three throws a penny, at thee,
To make thee a Purse: Seest thou this, bold bright blade?
This Sword shall shred thee as small unto the Grave,
As minc'd meat for a Pie. I'll set thee in Earth

All, save thy Head, and thy Right Arm at liberty,
To keep thy Hat off, while I question thee,
What? why? and whither thou wert going now,
With a Face, ready to break out with business?
And tell me truly, lest I dash't in pieces.

METAPHOR - Then, Basket, put thy Smiter up, and hear;
I dare not tell the Truth to a drawn Sword.

HILTS - 'Tis sheath'd, stand up, speak without fear or wit.

METAPHOR - I know not what they mean; but Constable Turfe
Sends here his Key, for Moneys in his Cubbard,
Which he must pay the Captain that was robb'd
This Morning. Smell you nothing?

HILTS - No, not I:
Thy Breeches yet are honest.

METAPHOR - As my Mouth.
Do you not smell a Rat? I tell you truth,
I think all's Knavery: For the Chanon whisper'd
Me in the Ear, when Turfe had gi'n me his Key,
By the same token to bring Mrs. Awdrey,
As sent for thither; and to say, John Clay
Is found, which is indeed to get the Wench
Forth for my Master, who is to be married
When she comes there: The Chanon has his Rules
Ready, and all there, to dispatch the matter.

TUB - Now on my life, this is the Chanon's plot!
Miles, I have heard all thy discourse to Basket.
Wilt thou be true, and I'll reward thee well,
To make me happy, in my Mistris Awdrey?

METAPHOR - Your Worship shall dispose of Metaphor,
Through all his parts, e'en from the sole o' the Head,
To the Crown o' the Foot, to manage of your service.

TUB - Then do thy Message to the Mistris Turfe,
Tell her thy token, bring the Money hither,
And likewise take young Awdrey to thy charge:
Which done, here, Metaphor, we will attend,
And intercept thee. And for thy Reward,
You two shall share the Money, I the Maid:
If any take offence, I'll make all good.

METAPHOR - But shall I have half the Money, Sir, in faith?

TUB - I, on my Squire-ship, shalt thou: and my Land.

METAPHOR - Then, if I make not, Sir, the clenliest scuse
To get her hither, and be then as careful
To keep her for you, as't were for my self,
Down o' your knees, and pray that honest Miles
May break his Neck ere he get o'er two Stiles.

ACT IV. SCENE III

TUB, HILTS.

TUB - Make haste then: we will wait here thy return.
This luck unlook'd for, hath reviv'd my hopes,
Which were opprest with a dark melancholy.
In happy time, we linger'd on the way,
To meet these Summons of a better sound,
Which are the Essence of my Soul's Content.

HILTS - This heartless fellow; shame to Serving-men;
Stain of all Liveries; what Fear makes him do!
How sordid, wretched, and unworthy things;
Betray his Masters Secrets, ope' the Closet
Of his Devices, force the foolish Justice,
Make way for your Love, plotting of his own:
Like him that digs a Trap, to catch another,
And falls into 't himself!

TUB - So wou'd I have it;
And hope 'twill prove a Jest to twit the Justice with.

HILTS - But that this poor white-liver'd Rogue should do't?
And meerly out of fear?

TUB - And hope of Money, Hilts.
A valiant Man will nibble at that Bait.

HILTS - Who, but a Fool, will refuse Money proffer'd?

TUB - And sent by so good chance. Pray Heaven he speed.

HILTS - If he come empty-handed, let him count
To go back empty-headed; I'll not leave him
So much of Brain in's Pate, with Pepper and Vinegar,
To be serv'd in for Sawce to a Calves Head.

TUB - Thou serv'st him rightly, Hilts.

HILTS - I'll seal as much
With my Hand, as I dare say now with my Tongue;
But if you get the Lass from Dargison,

What will you do with her?

TUB - We'll think o' that
When once we have her in possession, Governour.

PUPPY, METAPHOR, AWDREY.

PUPPY - You see we trust you, Mr. Metaphor,
With Mrs. Awdrey: 'pray you, use her well,
As a Gentlewoman should be us'd. For my part,
I do incline a little to the Serving-man;
We have been of a Coat—I had one like yours:
Till it did play me such a sleeveless Errand,
As I had nothing where to put mine Arms in,
And then I threw it off. Pray you, go before her,
Serving-man-like, and see that your Nose drop not.
As for example, you shall see me: Mark,
How I go a-fore her: So do you. Sweet Miles,
She, for her own part, is a Woman cares not
What Man can do unto her, in the way
Of Honesty, and good Manners. So farewel,
Fair Mrs. Awdrey: Farewel, Mr. Miles.
I ha' brought you thus far, onward o' your way:
I must go back now to make clean the Rooms,
Where my good Lady has been. Pray you commend me
To Bridegroom Clay; and bid him bear up stiff.

METAPHOR - Thank you, good Hannibal Puppy; I shall fit
The Leg of your Commands, with the straight Buskins
Of dispatch presently.

PUPPY - Farewel, fine Metaphor.

METAPHOR - Come, gentle Mistris, will you please to walk?

AWDREY - I love not to be led: I'd go alone.

METAPHOR - Let not the Mouse of my good meaning, Lady,
Be snap'd up in the Trap of your Suspicion,
To lose the Tail there, either of her Truth,
Or swallow'd by the Cat of Misconstruction.

AWDREY - You are too finical for me; speak plain, Sir.

TUB, AWDREY, HILTS, METAPHOR, LADY, POL-MARTIN. [To them.

TUB - Welcome again, my Awdrey: welcome, Love:
You shall with me; in faith deny me not.
I cannot brook the second hazard, Mistris.

AWDREY - Forbear, Squire Tub, as mine own Mother says,
I am not for your mowing. You'll be flown
Ere I be fledg'd.

HILTS - Hast thou the Money, Miles?

METAPHOR - Here are two Bags, there's Fifty Pound in each.

TUB - Nay, Awdrey, I possess you for this time:
Sirs, take that Coyn between you, and divide it.
My pretty Sweeting, give me now the leave
To challenge Love, and Marriage at your hands.

AWDREY - Now, out upon you, are you not asham'd?
What will my Lady say? In faith, I think
She was at our House: and I think she ask'd for you:
And I think she hit me i' th' teeth with you,
I thank her Ladyship: and I think she means
Not to go hence, till she has found you. How say you?

TUB - Was then my Lady Mother at your House?
Let's have a word aside.

AWDREY - Yes, Twenty words.

LADY TUB - 'Tis strange, a Motion, but I know not what,
Comes in my mind, to leave the way to Totten,
And turn to Kentish-town, again my Journey:
And see my Son, Pol-martin, with his Awdrey:
Ere while we left her at her Father's House:
And hath he thence remov'd her in such haste!
What shall I do? Shall I speak fair, or chide?

POL-MARTIN - Madam, your worthy Son, with dutious care,
Can govern his Affections: Rather than
Break off their Conference, some other way,
Pretending ignorance of what you know.

TUB - And this all, fair Awdrey: I am thine.

LADY TUB - Mine you were once, though scarcely now your own.

HILTS - 'Slid, my Lady! my Lady!

METAPHOR - Is this my Lady bright?

TUB - Madam, you took me now a little tardy.

LADY TUB - At Prayers, I think you were: What, so devout
Of late, that you will shrive you to all Confessors
You meet by chance? Come, go with me, good Squire,
And leave your Linnen: I have now a business,
And of importance, to impart unto you.

TUB - Madam, I pray you, spare me but an hour;
Please you to walk before, I follow you.

LADY TUB - It must be now, my business lies this way.

TUB - Will not an hour hence, Madam, excuse me?

LADY TUB - Squire, these Excuses argue more your Guilt.
You have some new Device now, to project,
Which the poor Tile-man scarce will thank you for.
What? will you go?

TUB - I ha' tane a charge upon me,
To see this Maid conducted to her Father,
Who, with the Chanon Hugh, stays her at Pancras,
To see her married to the same John Clay.

LADY TUB - 'Tis very well: but, Squire, take you no care.
I'll send Pol martin with her, for that Office:
You shall along with me; it is decreed.

TUB - I have a little business with a friend, Madam.

LADY TUB - That friend shall stay for you, or you for him.
Pol-martin, take the Maiden to your care:
Commend me to her Father.

TUB - I will follow you.

LADY TUB - Tut, tell not me of following.

TUB - I'll but speak a word.

LADY TUB - No whispering: you forget your self,
And make your Love too palpable: A Squire?
And think so meanly? fall upon a Cow-shard?
You know my mind. Come, I'll to Turfe's House,
And see for Dido, and our Valentine.
Pol-martin, look to your charge; I'll look to mine.

[They all go out but POL-MARTIN and AWDREY.

POL-MARTIN - I smile to think, after so many profers
This Maid hath had, she now should fall to me:
That I should have her in my custody:
'Twere but a mad trick to make the Essay,
And jump a Match with her immediately:
She's fair and handsome; and she's rich enough:
Both time and place minister fair occasion.
Have at it then: Fair Lady, can you love?

AWDREY - No Sir: What's that?

POL-MARTIN - A Toy which Women use.

AWDREY - If't be a Toy, it's good to play withal.

POL-MARTIN - We will not stand discoursing o' the Toy:
The way is short, please you to prov't, Mistris?

AWDREY - If you do mean to stand so long upon it.
I pray you let me give it a short cut, Sir.

POL-MARTIN - It's thus, fair Maid; Are you dispos'd to marry?

AWDREY - You are dispos'd to ask.

POL-MARTIN - Are you to grant?

AWDREY - Nay, now I see you are dispos'd indeed.

POL-MARTIN - I see the Wench wants but a little Wit;
And that Defect, her Wealth may well supply;
In plain terms, tell me, Will you have me, Awdrey?

AWDREY - In as plain terms, I tell you who would ha' me.
John Clay would ha' me, but he hath too hard Hands;
I like not him: Besides, he is a Thief.
And Justice Bramble, he would fain ha' catch'd me:
But the young Squire, he, rather than his life,
Would ha' me yet; and make me a Lady, he says,
And be my Knight; to do me true Knights service,
Before his Lady Mother. Can you make me
A Lady, would I ha' you?

POL-MARTIN - I can gi' you
A Silken Gown, and a Rich Petticoat:
And a French Hood. All Fools love to be brave:
I find her Humour, and I will pursue it.

LADY TUB, DAME TURFE, SQUIRE TUB, HILTS, PUPPY, CLAY.

LADY TUB - And, as I told thee, she was intercepted
By the Squire, here, my Son, and this bold Ruffian,
His Man; who safely would have carried her
Unto her Father, and the Chanon Hugh:
But for more care of the Security,
My Huisher hath her now in his grave charge.

DAME TURFE - Now on my Faith, and holy-dom, we are
Beholden to your Worship. She's a Girl,
A foolish Girl, and soon may tempted be:
But if this day pass well once o'er her Head,
I'll wish her trust to her self. For I have been
A very Mother to her, though I say it.

TUB - Madam, 'tis late, and Pancridge is i' your way:
I think your Ladyship forgets your self.

LADY TUB - Your mind runs much on Pancridge. Well, young Squire,
The black Oxe never trod yet o' your foot:
These idle Phant'sies will forsake you one day.
Come, Mrs. Turfe, will you go take a walk
Over the Fields to Pancridge, to your Husband?

DAME TURFE - Madam, I had been there an hour ago:
But that I waited on my Man Ball Puppy.
What, Ball, I say? I think the idle Slouch
De fall'n asleep i' the Barn, he stays so long.

PUPPY - Sattin, i' the name of Velvet-Sattin, Dame!
The Devil! O the Devil is in the Barn:
Help, help, a Legion —— Spirit-Legion
Is in the Barn! in every Straw a Devil.

DAME TURFE - Why do'st thou bawl so, Puppy? Speak, what ails thee?

PUPPY - My Name's Ball Puppy, I ha' seen the Devil
Among the Straw: O for a Cross! a Collop
Of Friar Bacon, or a conjuring stick
Of Doctor Faustus! Spirits are in the Barn.

TUB - How! Spirits in the Barn? Basket, go see.

HILTS - Sir, an' you were my Master ten times over,
And Squire to boot; I know, and you shall pardon me:
Send me 'mong Devils? I zee you love me not:
Hell be at their Game: I'll not trouble them.

TUB - Go see; I warrant thee there's no such matter.

HILTS - An' they were Giants, 'twere another matter.
But Devils! No, if I be torn in pieces,
What is your Warrant worth? I'll see the Fiend
Set fire o' the Barn, ere I come there.

DAME TURFE - Now all Zaints bless us, and if he be there,
He is an ugly Spright, I warrant.   PUPPY - As ever
Held Flesh-hook, Dame, or handled Fire-fork rather:
They have put me in a sweet pickle, Dame:
But that my Lady Valentine smells of Musk,
I should be asham'd to press into this presence.

LADY TUB - Basket, I pray thee see what is the Miracle!

TUB - Come, go with me: I'll lead. Why stand'st thou, Man?

HILTS - Cocks precious, Master, you are not mad indeed?
You will not go to Hell before your time?

TUB - Why art thou thus afraid?

HILTS - No, not afraid:
But by your leave, I'll come no near the Barn.

TUB - Puppy! wilt thou go with me?

PUPPY - How? go with you?
Whither, into the Barn? To whom, the Devil?
Or to do what there? to be torn 'mongst 'um?
Stay for my Master, the High Constable,
Or In-and-In, the Head-borough; let them go
Into the Barn with Warrant; seize the Fiend;
And set him in the Stocks for his ill rule:
'Tis not for me that am but Flesh and Blood,
To meddle with 'un. Vor I cannot, nor I wu' not.

LADY TUB - I pray thee, Tripoly, look, what is the matter?

TUB - That shall I, Madam.

HILTS - Heaven protect my Master.
I tremble every joynt till he be back.

PUPPY - Now, now, even now they are tearing him in pieces,
Now are they tossing of his Legs and Arms,
Like Loggets at a Pear-tree: I'll to the hole,
Peep in, and look whether he lives or dies.

HILTS - I would not be i' my Masters Coat for Thousands.

PUPPY - Then pluck it off, and turn thy self away.
O the Devil! the Devil! the Devil!

HILTS - Where, Man? where?

DAME TURFE - Alas, that ever we were born. So near too?

PUPPY - The Squire hath him in his hand, and leads him
Out by the Collar.

DAME TURFE - O, this is John Clay.

LADY TUB - John Clay at Pancrace, is there to be married.

TUB - This was the Spirit revell'd i' the Barn.

PUPPY - The Devil he was: was this he was crawling
Among the Wheat-straw? Had it been the Barley,
I should ha'tane him for the Devil in drink;
The Spirit of the Bride-Ale: But, poor John,
Tame John of Clay, that sticks about the Bung-hole —

HILTS - If this be all your Devil, I would take
In hand to conjure him: But hell take me,
If ere I come in a right Devil's walk,
If I can keep me out on't.

TUB - Well meant, Hilts.

LADY TUB - But how came Clay thus hid here i' the Straw,
When news was brought, to you all, he was at Pancridge;
And you believ'd it?

DAME TURFE - Justice Bramble's Man
Told me so, Madam: And by that same token,
And other things, he had away my Daughter,
And two seal'd Bags of Money.

LADY TUB - Where's the Squire:
Is he gone hence?

DAME TURFE - H' was here, Madam, but now.

CLAY - Is the Hue and Cry past by?

PUPPY - I, I, John Clay.

CLAY - And am I out of danger to be hang'd?

PUPPY - Hang'd, John? yes, sure; unless, as with the Proverb,

You mean to make the choice of your own Gallows.

CLAY - Nay, then all's well, hearing your news, Ball Puppy,
You ha' brought from Paddington, I e'en stole home here,
And thought to hide me in the Barn ere since.

PUPPY - O wonderful! and news was brought us here,
You were at Pancridge, ready to be married.

CLAY - No, faith, I ne'er was further than the Barn.

DAME TURFE - Haste, Puppy. Call forth Mistris Dido Wispe,
My Ladies Gentlewoman, to her Lady;
And call your self forth, and a Couple of Maids,
To wait upon me: we are all undone!
My Lady is undone! her fine young Son,
The Squire, is got away.

LADY TUB - Haste, haste, good Valentine.

DAME TURFE - And you, John Clay; you are undone too All!
My Husband is undone, by a true Key,
But a false Token: And my self's undone,
By parting with my Daughter, who'll be married
To some Body, that she should not, if we haste not.

ACT V. SCENE I

TUB, POL-MARTIN.

TUB – I pray thee, good Pol-martin, shew thy diligence,
And, faith, in both: Get her but so disguis'd,
The Chanon may not know her, and leave me
To plot the rest: I will expect thee here.

POL-MARTIN - You shall, Squire. I'll perform it with all care,
If all my Ladies Ward-robe will disguise her.
Come, Mistris Awdrey.

AWDREY - Is the Squire gone?

POL-MARTIN - He'll meet us by and by, where he appointed:
You shall be brave anon, as none shall know you.

ACT V. SCENE II

[To them.

CLENCH, MEDLAY, PAN, SCRIBEN, TUB, HILTS

CLENCH – I wonder where the Queens High Constable is!
I vear they ha' made 'un away.

MEDLAY - No zure; the Justice
Dare not conzent to that. He'll zee 'un forth coming.

TO-PAN - He must, vor we can all take Corpulent Oath,
We zaw 'un go in there.

SCRIBEN - I, upon Record!
The Clock dropt Twelve at Maribone.

MEDLAY - You are right, D'oge!
Zet down to a minute, now 'tis a'most vowre.

CLENCH - Here comes Squire Tub.

SCRIBEN - And's Governour, Mr. Basket
Hilts, do you know 'un, a valiant wise vellow!
Az tall a Man on his Hands, as goes on veet.
Bless you, Mass' Basket.

HILTS - Thank you, good D'oge.

TUB - Who's that?

HILTS - D'oge Scriben, the great Writer, Sir, of Chalcot.

TUB - And, who the rest?

HILTS - The wisest Heads o' the Hundred.
Medlay the Joyner, Head-borough of Islington,
Pan of Belsize, and Clench, the Leach of Hamsted,
The High Constables Counsel, here, of Finsbury.

TUB - Prezent me to 'em, Hilts, Squire Tub of Totten.

HILTS - Wise Men of Finsbury, make place for a Squire,
I bring to your acquaintance, Tub of Totten.
Squire Tub, my Master, loves all Men of Vertue,
And longs (as one would zay) till he be one on you.

CLENCH - His Worship's wel'cun to our Company:
Would 't were wiser for 'un.

TO-PAN - Here be some on us,
Are call'd the Witty Men, over a Hundred.

SCRIBEN - And zome a Thousand, when the Muster-day comes.

TUB - I long (as my Man Hilts said, and my Governour)
To be adopt in your Society.
Can any Man make a Masque here i' this Company?

TO-PAN - A Masque! what's that?

SCRIBEN - A Mumming, or a Shew,
With Vizards and fine Clothes.

CLENCH - A Disguise, Neighbour,
Is the true word: There stands the Man can do't, Sir:
Medlay the Joyner, In-and-In of Islington,
The only Man at a Disguise in Middlesex.

TUB - But who shall write it?

HILTS - Scriben, the great Writer.

SCRIBEN - He'll do't alone, Sir; he will joyn with no man:
Though he be a Joyner, in design he calls it,
He must be sole Inventer: In-and-In
Draws with no other in's Project, he'll tell you,
It cannot else be feazeable, or conduce:
Those are his ruling words? Pleaze you to hear 'un?

TUB - Yes, Mr. In-and-In, I have heard of you.

MEDLAY - I can do nothing, I.

CLENCH - He can do all, Sir.

MEDLAY - They'll tell you so.

TUB - I'ld have a Toy presented,
A Tale of a Tub, a Story of my self,
You can express a Tub.

MEDLAY - If it conduce
To the Design, whate'er is feazeable:
I can express a Wash-house (if need be),
With a whole Pedigree of Tubs.

TUB - No, one
Will be enough to note our Name and Family:
Squire Tub of Totten, and to shew my Adventures
This very day. I'ld have it in Tubs-Hall,
At Totten-Court, my Lady Mothers House;
My House indeed; for I am Heir to it.

MEDLAY - If I might see the place, and had survey'd it,

I could say more: For all Invention, Sir,
Comes by degrees, and on the view of Nature,
A world of things concur to the design,
Which make it feazible, if Art conduce.

TUB - You say well, witty Mr. In-and-In.
How long ha' you studied, Ingine?

MEDLAY - Since I first
Joyn'd, or did in-lay in Wit, some vorty year.

TUB - A pretty time! Basket, go you and wait
On Master In-and-In, to Totten-Court,
And all the other wise Masters: Shew 'em the Hall:
And taste the Language of the Buttery to 'em:
Let 'em see all the Tubs about the House,
That can raise Matter, till I come — which shall be
Within an Hour, at least.

CLENCH - It will be glorious,
If In-and-In will undertake it, Sir:
He has a monstrous Medlay Wit o' his own.

TUB - Spare for no cost, either in Boards or Hoops,
To architect your Tub: Ha' you ne'er a Cooper
At London, call'd Vitruvius? Send for him;
Or old John Haywood, call him to you, to help.

SCRIBEN - He scorns the Motion, trust to him alone.

ACT V. SCENE III

LADY TUB, TUB, DAME TURFE, CLAY, PUPY, WISPE, PREAMBLE, TURFE.

LADY TUB - O, here's the Squire! you slipp'd us finely, Son!
These Manners to your Mother, will commend you;
But in another Age, not this: Well, Tripoly,
Your Father, good Sir Peter, (rest his Bones)
Would not ha' done this: Where's my Huisher Martin?
And your fair Mrs. Awdrey?

TUB - I not see 'em,
No Creature, but the Four Wise Masters here,
Of Finsbury Hundred, came to cry their Constable,
Who, they do say, is lost.

DAME TURFE - My Husband lost?
And my fond Daughter lost? I fear me too.
Where is your Gentleman, Madam? Poor John Clay,

Thou hast lost thy Awdrey.

CLAY - I ha' lost my Wits,
My little Wits, good Mother; I am distracted.

PUPPY - And I have lost my Mistris Dido Wispe,
Who frowns upon her Puppy, Hannibal.
Loss! loss on every side! a publick loss!
Loss o' my Master! loss of his Daughter! loss
Of Favour, Friends, my Mistris! loss of all!

PREAMBLE - What Cry is this?

TURFE - My Man speaks of some loss.

PUPPY - My Master is found: Good luck, and't be thy will,
Light on us all.

DAME TURFE - O Husband, are you alive?
They said you were lost.

TURFE - Where's Justice Bramble's Clerk?
Had he the Money that I sent for?

DAME TURFE - Yes,
Two Hours ago, two Fifty Pounds in Silver,
And Awdrey too.

TURFE - Why Awdrey? who sent for her?

DAME TURFE - You, Master Turfe, the Fellow said.

TURFE - He lyed.
I am cozen'd, robb'd, undone: Your Man's a Thief,
And run away with my Daughter, Mr. Bramble,
And with my Money.

LADY TUB - Neighbour Turfe, have patience,
I can assure you that your Daughter is safe,
But for the Monies, I know nothing of.

TURFE - My Money is my Daughter, and my Daughter
She is my Money, Madam.

PREAMBLE - I do wonder
Your Ladyship comes to know any thing
In these affairs.

LADY TUB - Yes, Justice Bramble,
I met the Maiden i' the Fields by chance,
I' the Squire's Company, my Son: How he

Lighted upon her, himself best can tell.

TUB - I intercepted her, as coming hither,
To her Father, who sent for her, by Miles Metaphor,
Justice Preamble's Clerk. And had your Ladyship
Not hindred it, I had paid fine Mr. Justice,
For his young Warrant, and new Purs'yvant,
He serv'd it by this morning.

PREAMBLE - Know you that, Sir?

LADY TUB - You told me, Squire, a quite other Tale,
But I believ'd you not, which made me send
Awdrey another way, by my Pol-martin:
And take my Journey back to Kentish-town,
Where we found John Clay hidden i' the Barn,
To scape the Hue and Cry: and here he is.

TURFE - John Clay agen! nay, then—set Cock a hoop:
I ha' lost no Daughter, nor no Money, Justice.
John Clay shall pay. I'll look to you now, John.
Vaith, out it must, as good at night as morning.
I am e'en as vull as a Piper's Bag, with Joy;
Or a great Gun upon Carnation-day!
I could weep Lyons Tears to see you, John.
'Tis but two vifty pounds I ha' ventur'd for you:
But now I ha' you, you shall pay whole hundred.
Run from your Burroughs, Son! Faith, e'en be hang'd.
An' you once earth your self, John, i' the Barn,
I ha' no Daughter vor you: Who did verret 'un?

DAME TURFE - My Ladies Son, the Squire here, vetch'd 'un out.
Puppy had put us all in such a vright,
We thought the Devil was i' the Barn; and no body
Durst venture o' 'un.

TURFE - I am now resolv'd
Who shall ha' my Daughter.

DAME TURFE - Who?

TURFE - He best deserves her.
Here comes the Vicar. Chanon Hugh, we ha' vound
John Clay agen! the matter's all come round.

ACT V. SCENE IV

[To them.
CHANON HUGH.

SIR HUGH - Is Metaphor return'd yet?

PREAMBLE - All is turn'd
Here to confusion: We ha' lost our Plot;
I fear my Man is run away with the Money,
And Clay is found, in whom old Turfe is sure
To save his Stake.

SIR HUGH - What shall we do then, Justice?

PREAMBLE - The Bride was met i' the young Squire's hands.

SIR HUGH - And what's become of her?

PREAMBLE - None here can tell.

TUB - Was not my Mothers Man, Pol-martin, with you?
And a strange Gentlewoman in his company,
Of late here, Chanon?

SIR HUGH - Yes, and I dispatch'd 'em.

TUB - Dispatch'd 'em! how do you mean?

SIR HUGH - Why, married 'em.
As they desir'd; but now.

TUB - And do you know
What you ha' done, Sir Hugh?

SIR HUGH - No harm, I hope.

TUB - You have ended all the Quarrel: Awdrey is married.

LADY TUB - Married! to whom?

TURFE - My Daughter Awdrey married,
And she not know of it!

DAME TURFE - Nor her Father, or Mother!

LADY TUB - Whom hath she married?

TUB - Your Pol-martin, Madam.
A Groom was never dreamt of.

TURFE - Is he a Man?

LADY TUB - That he is, Turfe, and a Gentleman, I ha' made him.

DAME TURFE - Nay, an' he be a Gentleman, let her shift.

SIR HUGH - She was so brave, I knew her not, I swear;
And yet I married her by her own name.
But she was so disguis'd, so Lady-like,
I think she did not know her self the while!
I married 'em as a meer pair of strangers:
And they gave out themselves for such.

LADY TUB - I wish 'em
Much Joy, as they have given me hearts ease.

TUB - Then, Madam, I'll intreat you now remit
Your Jealousie of me; and please to take
All this good Company home with you to Supper:
We'll have a merry night of it, and laugh.

LADY TUB - A right good motion, Squire; which I yield to:
And thank them to accept it. Neighbour Turfe,
I'll have you merry, and your Wife: And you,
Sir Hugh, be pardon'd this your happy Error.
By Justice Preamble, your Friend and Patron.

PREAMBLE - If the young Squire can pardon it, I do.

ACT V. SCENE V

[Tarry behind. PUPPY, DIDO, SIR HUGH.

PUPPY - Stay, my dear Dido, and good Vicar Hugh,
We have a business with you: In short, this,
If you dare knit another pair of Strangers,
Dido, of Carthage, and her Countrey-man,
Stout Hannibal stands to't. I have ask'd consent,
And she hath granted.

SIR HUGH - But saith Dido so?

DIDO - From what Ball-Hanny hath said, I dare not go.

SIR HUGH - Come in then, I'll dispatch you. A good Supper
Would not be lost, good Company, good Discourse;
But above all, where Wit hath any source.

ACT V. SCENE VI

POL-MARTIN, AWDREY, TUB, LADY, PREAMBLE, TURFE, DAME TURFE, CLAY.

POL-MARTIN - After the hoping of your pardon, Madam,
For many Faults committed. Here my Wife,
And I do stand, expecting your mild Doom.

LADY TUB - I wish thee Joy, Pol-martin; and thy Wife
As much, Mrs. Pol-martin. Thou hast trick'd her
Up very fine, me thinks.

POL-MARTIN - For that, I made
Bold with your Ladyships Wardrobe, but have trespass'd
Within the limits of your leave—I hope.

LADY TUB - I give her what she wears. I know all Women
Love to be fine. Thou hast deserv'd it of me:
I am extreamly pleas'd with thy good Fortune.
Welcome, good Justice Preamble; And Turfe,
Look merrily on your Daughter: She has married
A Gentleman.

TURFE - So me thinks. I dare not touch her,
She is so fine: yet I will say, God bless her.

DAME TURFE - And I too, my fine Daughter. I could love her
Now, twice as well, as if Clay had her.

TUB - Come, come, my Mother is pleas'd: I pardon all.
Pol-martin, in, and wait upon my Lady.
Welcome good Guests: see Supper be serv'd in,
With all the Plenty of the House, and Worship.
I must confer with Mr. In-and-In,
About some Alterations in my Masque:
Send Hilts out to me; Bid him bring the Council
Of Finsbury hither. I'll have such a night
Shall make the Name of Totten-Court Immortal:
And be Recorded to Posterity.

ACT V. SCENE VII

TUB, MEDLAY, CLENCH, PAN, SCRIBEN, HILTS..

TUB – O Mr. In-and-In, what ha' you done?

MEDLAY - Survey'd the Place, Sir, and design'd the Ground,
Or stand still of the work: And this it is.
First, I have fixed in the Earth, a Tub;
And an old Tub, like a Salt-Petre-Tub,
Preluding by your Father's Name, Sir Peter.
And the Antiquity of your House and Family,

Original from Salt-Petre.   TUB - Good yfaith,
You ha' shewn Reading, and Antiquity here, Sir.

MEDLAY - I have a little knowledge in design,
Which I can vary, Sir, to Infinito.

TUB - Ad Infinitum, Sir, you mean.

MEDLAY - I do.
I stand not on my Latine, I'll invent;
But I must be alone then, joyn'd with no Man.
This we do call the Stand-still of our work.

TUB - Who are those we, you now joyn'd to your self?

MEDLAY - I mean my self still, in the Plural Number,
And out of this we raise our Tale of a Tub.

TUB - No, Mr. In-and-In, my Tale of a Tub,
By your leave, I am Tub, the Tale's of me,
And my Adventures! I am Squire Tub,
Subjectum Fabulæ.

MEDLAY - But I the Author.

TUB - The Workman, Sir! the Artificer! I grant you.
So Skelton-Laureat, was of Elinour Bumming;
But she the Subject of the Rout and Tunning.

CLENCH - He has put you to it, Neighbour In-and-In.

TO-PAN - Do not dispute with him, he still will win.
That pays for all.

SCRIBEN - Are you revis'd o' that?
A Man may have Wit, and yet put off his Hat.

MEDLAY - Now, Sir, this Tub, I will have capt with Paper:
A fine Oyl'd Lantern-paper, that we use.

TO-PAN - Yes, every Barber, every Cutler has it.

MEDLAY - Which in it doth contain the light to the business.
And shall with the very Vapour of the Candle,
Drive all the motions of our Matter about:
As we present 'em. For Example, first,
The Worshipful Lady Tub.

TUB - Right Worshipful,
I pray you, I am Worshipful my self.

MEDLAY - Your Squireship's Mother, passeth by (her Huisher, Mr. POL-MARTIN, bare-headed before her) In her Velvet Gown.

TUB - But how shall the Spectators,
As it might be, I, or Hilts, know 'tis my Mother?
Or that Pol-martin, there, that walks before her.

MEDLAY - O we do nothing, if we clear not that.

CLENCH - You ha' seen none of his Works, Sir?

TO-PAN - All the postures
Of the Train'd Bands o' the Countrey.

SCRIBEN - All their Colours.

TO-PAN - And all their Captains.

CLENCH - All the Cries o' the City:
And all the Trades i' their Habits.

SCRIBEN - He has his Whistle
Of Command: Seat of Authority!
And Virge to interpret, tip'd with Silver, Sir,
You know not him.

TUB - Well, I will leave all to him.

MEDLAY - Give me the brief o' your Subject. Leave the whole
State of the thing to me.

HILTS - Supper is ready, Sir.
My Lady calls for you.

TUB - I'll send it you in writing.

MEDLAY - Sir, I will render feazible, and facile,
What you expect.

TUB - Hilts, be't your care,
To see the Wise of Finsbury made welcome:
Let 'em want nothing. Is old Rosin sent for?

[The SQUIRE goes out.

HILTS - He's come within.

SCRIBEN - Lord! what a world of business
The Squire dispatches!

MEDLAY - He is a learned Man:

I think there are but vew o' the Inns o' Court,
Or the Inns o' Chancery like him.

[The rest follow.

CLENCH - Care to fit 'un then.

JACK, HILTS.

JACK - Yonder's another Wedding, Master Basket,
Brought in by Vicar Hugh.

HILTS - What are they, Jack?

JACK - The High Constable's Man, Ball Hanny; and Mrs. Wispes, Wispe
Our Ladies Woman.

HILTS - And are the Table merry?

JACK - There's a young Tile-maker makes all laugh;
He will not eat his Meat, but crys at th' Board,
He shall be hang'd.

HILTS - He has lost his Wench already:
As good be hang'd.

JACK - Was she that is Pol-martin,
Our Fellows Mistris, wench to that Sneak-John?

HILTS - I faith, Black Jack, he should have been her Bridegroom:
But I must go to wait o' my Wise Masters.

Jack, you shall wait on me, and see the Mask anon:
I am half Lord Chamberlain i' my Master's absence.

JACK - Shall we have a Mask? Who makes it?

HILTS - In-and-In.

2 GROOMS.

1st GROOM - Come, give us in the great Chair, for my Lady,
And set it there: and this for Justice Bramble.

2nd GROOM - This for the Squire my Master, on the right hand.

1st GROOM - And this for the High Constable.

2nd GROOM - This his Wife.

1st GROOM - Then for the Bride and Bridegroom here, Pol-martin.

2nd GROOM - And she Pol-martin, at my Ladies Feet.

1st GROOM - Right.

2nd GROOM - And beside them Mr. Hannibal Puppy.

1st GROOM - And his she Puppy, Mrs. Wispe that was:
Here's all are in the Note.

2nd GROOM - No, Mr. Vicar:
The petty Chanon Hugh.

1st GROOM - And Cast-by Clay:
There they are all.

TUB - Then cry a Hall, a Hall!
'Tis merry in Tottenham Hall, when Beards wag all.
Come, Father Rosin, with your Fiddle now,

[Loud Musick.
And two tall-toters: Flourish to the Masque.

ACT V. SCENE X

LADY, PREAMBLE before her. TUB, TURFE, DAME TURFE, POL-MARTIN, AWDREY, PUPPY, WISPE,
HUGH, CLAY. All take their Seats. HILTS waits on the by.

LADY TUB - Neighbours all welcome: Now doth Totten-Hall
Shew like a Court: And hence shall first be call'd so.
Your witty short Confession, Mr. Vicar,
Within, hath been the Prologue, and hath open'd
Much to my Son's Device, his Tale of a Tub.

TUB - Let my Masque shew it self: And In-and-In,
The Architect, appear: I hear the Whistle.

[HILTS - Peace.

[MEDLAY appears above the Curtain.

MEDLAY - Thus rise I first, in my light Linnen Breeches,
To run the meaning over in short Speeches.
Here is a Tub, a Tub of Totten-Court:
An ancient Tub, hath call'd you to this sport:
His Father was a Knight, the rich Sir Peter;
Who got his Wealth by a Tub, and by Salt-Petre:
And left all to his Lady Tub, the Mother
Of this bold Squire Tub, and to no other.
Now of this Tub, and's Deeds, not done in Ale,
Observe, and you shall see the very Tale.

[He draws the Curtain, and discovers the top of the TUB.

The First Motion.

[Ha' peace. Loud Musick.

MEDLAY - Here Chanon Hugh first brings to Totten-Hall
The High Constable's Council, tells the Squire all;
Which, though discover'd (give the Devil his due:)
The Wise of Finsbury do still pursue.
Then with the Justice doth he counterplot,
And his Clerk Metaphor, to cut that knot:
Whilst Lady Tub, in her sad Velvet Gown,
Missing her Son, doth seek him up and down.

TUB - With her Pol-martin bare before her.

MEDLAY - Yes,
I have exprest it here in Figure, and Mistris
Wispe, her Woman, holding up her Train.

TUB - I' the next page, report your second Strain.

The Second Motion.

[HILTS - Ha' peace.

Loud Musick.

MEDLAY - Here the High Constable, and Sages walk
To Church, the Dame, the Daughter, Bride-maids talk
Of Wedding-business; till a Fellow in comes,
Relates the Robbery of one Captain Thum's:
Chargeth the Bridegroom with it: Troubles all,
And gets the Bride; who in the Hands doth fall
Of the bold Squire; but thence soon is tane
By the sly Justice, and his Clerk profane,
In shape of Pursuyvant; which he not long
Holds, but betrays all with his trembling Tongue:
As truth will break out, and shew, &c.

TUB - O, thou hast made him kneel there in a corner,
I see now: There is simple Honour for you, Hilts!

HILTS - Did I not make him to confess all to you?

TUB - True, In-and-In hath done you right, you see.
Thy Third, I pray thee, witty In-and-In.

CLENCH - The Squire commends 'un. He doth like all well.

TO-PAN - He cannot chuse. This is Gear made to sell.

The Third Motion.

[HILTS - Ha' peace. Loud Musick.

MEDLAY - The careful Constable, here drooping comes,
In his deluded search of Captain Thum's.
Puppy brings word, his Daughter's run away
With the tall Serving-man. He frights Groom Clay
Out of his Wits. Returneth then the Squire,
Mocks all their Pains, and gives Fame out a Lyar,
For falsly charging Clay, when 'twas the Plot
Of subtle Bramble, who had Awdrey got,
Into his hand, by his winding device.
The Father makes a Rescue in a trice:
And with his Daughter, like Saint George on foot,
Comes home triumphing, to his dear Heart root.
And tells the Lady Tub, whom he meets there,
Of her Son's Courtesies, the Batchelor.
Whose words had made 'em fall the Hue and Cry.
When Captain Thum's coming to ask him, why
He had so done? He cannot yield him cause:
But so he runs his Neck into the Laws.

The Fourth Motion.

[HILTS - Ha' peace. Loud Musick.

MEDLAY - The Laws, who have a Noose to crak his Neck,
As Justice Bramble tells him, who doth peck
A Hundreth Pound out of his Purse, that comes
Like his Teeth from him, unto Captain Thum's.
Thum's is the Vicar in a false disguise:
And employs Metaphor to fetch this Prize.
Who tells the Secret unto Basket-Hilts,
For fear of beating. This the Squire quilts
Within his Cap; and bids him but purloin
The Wench for him: They Two shall share the Coyn.
Which the sage Lady, in her 'foresaid Gown,

Breaks off, returning unto Kentish-town,
To seek her Wispe; taking the Squire along,
Who finds Clay John, as hidden in Straw throng.

HILTS - O, how am I beholden to the Inventer,
That would not, on Record, against me enter!
My slackness here, to enter in the Barn:
Well, In-and-In, I see thou canst discern!

TUB - On with your last, and come to a Conclusion.

The Fifth Motion.

[HILTS - Ha' peace.   Loud Musick

MEDLAY - The last is known, and needs but small infusion
Into your Memories, by leaving in
These Figures, as you sit. I, In-and-In,
Present you with the Show: First, of a Lady
Tub, and her Son, of whom this Masque here, made I.
Then Bridegroom Pol, and Mistris Pol the Bride:
With the Sub-Couple, who sit them beside.

TUB - That only Verse I alter'd for the better, eufonia gratiâ.

MEDLAY - Then Justice Bramble, with Sir Hugh the Chanon:
And the Bride's Parents, which I will not stan' on,
Or the lost Clay, with the recovered Giles:
Who thus unto his Master, him 'conciles,
On the Squire's Word, to pay old Turfe his Club,
And so doth end our Tale here, of a Tub.

EPILOGUE

SQUIRE TUB - This Tale of me, the Tub of Totten-Court,
A Poet first invented for your Sport.
Wherein the Fortune of most empty Tubs
Rowling in Love, are shewn; and with what Rubs
W' are commonly encountred: When the Wit
Of the whole Hundred so opposeth it.
Our petty Chanon's Forked Plot in chief,
Sly Justice Arts, with the High Constable's Brief,
And brag Commands; my Lady Mothers Care,
And her Pol-martin's Fortune; with the rare
Fate of poor John, thus tumbled in the Cask;
Got In-and-In to gi't you in a Masque:
That you be pleas'd, who come to see a Play,
With those that hear, and mark not what we say.
Wherein the Poets Fortune is, I fear,

Still to be early up, but ne'er the near.

Ben Jonson was born on either (by most accounts) June 9th or June 11th, 1572 in Westminster, London.

Jonson later recounted that his father (who died before he was born) had been a prosperous Protestant landowner until the reign of "Bloody Mary" and had suffered imprisonment and the forfeiture of his wealth during that monarch's attempt to restore England to Catholicism. On Elizabeth's accession he was freed and was able to travel to London to become a clergyman. His widowed mother remarried two years after his death.

Jonson's education began in a small church school attached to St Martin-in-the-Fields parish, and at the age of about seven he secured a place at Westminster School. It is attributed that a family friend paid for his studies at Westminster, where the antiquarian, historian, topographer, and officer of arms, William Camden was a master. Pupil and master became great friends, and Camden's broad range of interests and teachings had a great influence on Jonson throughout Camden's life.

On leaving Westminster School, Cambridge beckoned but instead Jonson was apprenticed to his bricklayer stepfather. After this apprenticeship Jonson travelled to the Netherlands and signed up as a volunteer with the English regiments of Francis Vere (1560–1609), in Flanders.

The later Hawthornden Manuscripts (1619), that recorded the conversations between Ben Jonson and the poet William Drummond of Hawthornden (1585–1649), report that, when in Flanders, Jonson engaged, fought, and killed an enemy soldier in single combat, and took for trophies the weapons of the vanquished soldier. After his military activity on the Continent, Jonson returned to England and worked as an actor and a playwright.

As an actor, Jonson was the protagonist "Hieronimo" (Geronimo) in the play The Spanish Tragedy, by Thomas Kyd (1558–94), the first revenge tragedy in English literature.

Naturally certainty in the details of these times is difficult. He appears to have married a "a shrew, yet honest" woman, sometimes attributed as Ann(e) Lewis at the church of St Magnus-the-Matyr near London Bridge in 1594 though other accounts give November 1593 as the date of the death of their 6 month old daughter Mary (immortalised in the heart breaking poem "On My First Daughter"), suggesting the marriage was somewhat earlier.

By the summer of 1597, Jonson had a fixed engagement in the Admiral's Men, performing under Philip Henslowe, then the leading producer for the English public theatre, at The Rose. Jonson appears not to have been much of an actor but showed potential as a writer.

His early forays as playwright were tragedies but none are recorded as surviving. An undated comedy 'The Case is Altered' is thought to be the earliest.

Jonson was not shy of causing controversy and many of his views courted it easily. In 1597 a play which he co-wrote with Thomas Nashe, The Isle of Dogs, was suppressed after causing great offence. Warrants for the arrest of Jonson and Nashe were issued by Queen Elizabeth I's interrogator, Richard Topcliffe.

Jonson was jailed in Marshalsea Prison and charged with "Leude and mutynous behavior", while Nashe managed to escape to Great Yarmouth. Two of the actors, Gabriel Spenser and Robert Shaw, were also imprisoned.

In 1598 Jonson produced his first great success, Every Man in His Humour, capitalising on the fashion for comedic plays which George Chapman had begun with An Humorous Day's Mirth. A certain William Shakespeare was among the first actors to be cast.

A year later, Jonson was again briefly imprisoned, this time in Newgate Prison, for killing Gabriel Spenser in a duel on 22 September 1598 in Hogsden Fields. Tried on a charge of manslaughter, Jonson would plead guilty but be released by benefit of clergy, a legal ploy through which he gained leniency by reciting a brief bible verse (the neck-verse), forfeiting his 'goods and chattels' and being branded on his left thumb.

But during his time Jonson's faith was to play a further complicating part in this difficult situation. Brought up in the Protestant faith, he had maintained an interest in Catholic doctrine throughout his adult life and, at this perilous time when a religious war with Spain was expected and persecution of Catholics was intensifying, he converted to the Catholic faith in October 1598 (while he was still on remand in Newgate). It was a unique combination of events and obviously a difficult choice.

It has been suggested that the conversion was instigated by Father Thomas Wright, a former Jesuit priest who had resigned from the order over his acceptance of Queen Elizabeth's right to rule in England. Wright, although placed under house arrest on the orders of Lord Burghley, was permitted to minister to the inmates of London prisons. It may have been that Jonson, fearing that his trial would go against him, was seeking the unequivocal absolution that Catholicism could offer if he were sentenced to death. Or, almost equally, he could have been looking to personal advantage from accepting conversion since Father Wright's protector, the Earl of Essex, was among those who might hope to rise to influence after the succession of a new monarch. The argument was that the royal succession, from the childless Elizabeth, had not been settled and Essex's Catholic allies were hopeful that a sympathetic ruler might attain the throne.

Either way, Jonson was now released and his artistic life was the main channel of his activity. This continued to flower and in 1599, Every Man Out of His Humour, was performed on stage. When it was published it proved popular and went through several editions.

Jonson's other work for the theatre in the last years of Elizabeth I's reign was marked by fighting and controversy. Cynthia's Revels was produced by the Children of the Chapel Royal at Blackfriars Theatre in 1600. It satirised both John Marston, who Jonson believed had accused him of lustfulness, possibly in Histrio-Mastix, and Thomas Dekker. Jonson attacked the two poets again in 1601's Poetaster. Dekker responded with Satiromastix, subtitled "the untrussing of the humorous poet".

This "War of the Theatres" seems to have ended with reconciliation on all sides. Jonson collaborated with Dekker on a pageant welcoming James I to England in 1603 although Drummond reports that Jonson called Dekker a rogue. Marston dedicated The Malcontent to Jonson.

Tragically, that same 1603, Benjamin Jonson, his eldest son, died of Bubonic plague at the age of seven; to lament and honour the dead boy, Jonson wrote the elegiac On My First Sonne.

With the new King, James I, on the throne Jonson quickly saw the need for and demand for masques and entertainments which was also promoted by both the king and his consort Anne of Denmark. In addition to his popularity on the public stage and in the royal hall, he enjoyed the patronage of aristocrats such as Elizabeth Sidney (daughter of Sir Philip Sidney) and Lady Mary Wroth. This connection with the Sidney family provided the impetus for one of Jonson's most famous lyrics, the country house poem To Penshurst.

In February 1603 John Manningham reported that Jonson was living at Robert Townsend's, son of Sir Roger Townshend, and "scorns the world." This provides a plausible and reasonable explanation as to why his troubles with English authorities continued. That same year he was questioned by the Privy Council about Sejanus, a politically themed play about corruption in the Roman Empire. Conviction, and certainly not expedience alone, sustained Jonson's faith during the troublesome twelve years he remained a Catholic. His stance received attention beyond the state intolerance to which most faithful followers were exposed. That first draft of Sejanus was banned for "popery", and did not re-appear until the offending passages were cut.

At the same time, Jonson pursued a more prestigious career, writing masques for James's court. The Satyr (1603) and The Masque of Blackness (1605) are two of about two dozen masques which Jonson wrote for James or for Queen Anne; The Masque of Blackness was praised by Algernon Charles Swinburne as the consummate example of this now-extinct genre, which mingled speech, dancing, and spectacle.

In 1605 Jonson collaborated with Chapman on Eastward Ho, a play whose anti-Scottish sentiment landed both authors in jail for a short time to bring home to them the authorities displeasure with their work. Shortly after he was, unfortunately, present at a supper party attended by most of the Gunpowder Plot conspirators.

With the plot's discovery he seems to have avoided further imprisonment by volunteering what he knew to the investigator Robert Cecil and the Privy Council. Father Thomas Wright, who heard Fawkes's confession, was known to Jonson from prison in 1598 and Cecil may have directed him to bring the priest before the council, as a witness.

Now, in January 1606, Jonson (with his wife Anne) appeared before the Consistory Court to answer a charge of recusancy, with Jonson additionally accused of allowing his fame as a Catholic to "seduce" citizens to the cause. This was a serious matter, especially as the Gunpowder Plot was only a few moths before, but he explained that his failure to take communion was only because he had not found sound theological endorsement for the practice. By paying a fine of thirteen shillings he escaped the more serious penalties available to the authorities. His habit was to slip outside during the sacrament, a common routine at the time—indeed it was one followed by Queen Anne, herself —to show political loyalty whilst not offending the conscience. Leading church figures, including John Overall, Dean of St Paul's, were directed to win Jonson back to orthodoxy, but these overtures met no success.

Jonson's poetry, as is his drama, is informed by his classical learning. Some of his better-known poems are close translations of Greek or Roman models; all display a careful attention to form and style that often came naturally to those trained in classics. Jonson largely avoided debate about rhyme and meter that had consumed other Elizabethan classicists. Accepting both rhyme and stress, Jonson used them to mimic the classical qualities of simplicity, restraint, and precision.

In May 1610 King Henri IV of France, a Catholic monarch respected in England for tolerance towards Protestants, was assassinated, purportedly in the name of the Pope, and this seems to have been the immediate cause of Jonson's decision to rejoin the Church of England. He did this in flamboyant style, pointedly drinking a full chalice of communion wine at the eucharist to demonstrate his renunciation of the Catholic rite, in which the priest alone drinks the wine. Despite this very public display his interest in Catholic belief and practice remained with him until his death.

On ensuing projects he collaborated, not always peacefully, with the designer Inigo Jones. For example, Jones designed the scenery for Jonson's masque Oberon, the Faery Prince performed at Whitehall on 1 January 1611 in which Prince Henry, eldest son of James I, appeared in the title role.

Perhaps partly as a result of this new career, Jonson gave up writing plays for the public theatres for a decade. He later told Drummond that he had made less than two hundred pounds on all his plays together.

The period between 1605 and 1620 may mow be viewed as Jonson's golden period. By 1616 he had produced all the plays on which his present reputation as a dramatist is based, including the tragedy Catiline (acted and printed 1611), which achieved limited success, and the comedies Volpone, (acted 1605, printed in 1607), Epicoene, or the Silent Woman (1609), The Alchemist (1610), Bartholomew Fair (1614) and The Devil is an Ass (1616). The Alchemist and Volpone were immediately successful. Epicoene, Bartholomew Fair and (to a lesser extent) The Devil is an Ass have, in modern times, achieved a greater degree of recognition. During this period his life was more settled and without so much of the excess and controversy of former years but, despite this success, his financial security was still not assured.

In 1616 Jonson received a yearly pension of 100 marks (about £60), and was also appointed as Poet Laureate (though this Post was long standing it was, at the time, an unofficial position). This sign of royal favour may have encouraged him to publish the first volume of the folio collected edition of his works that year. Other volumes were to follow much later.

Included in the 1615 folio are "Epigrams", a genre popular among late-Elizabethan and Jacobean audiences, although Jonson was perhaps the only poet of his time to work in its full classical range. The epigrams explore various attitudes, most from the satiric stock of the day: complaints against women, courtiers, and spies abound. The condemnatory poems are short and anonymous; Jonson's epigrams of praise, including a famous poem to Camden and lines to Lucy Harington, are longer and are mostly addressed to specific individuals. Although it is included among the epigrams, "On My First Sonne" is neither satirical nor very short; the poem, intensely personal and deeply felt, typifies a genre that would evolve itself to be called "lyric poetry." Jonson's poems of "The Forest" also appeared in the first folio. Most of the fifteen poems are addressed to Jonson's aristocratic supporters, but the most famous are his country-house poem "To Penshurst" and the poem "To Celia" ("Come, my Celia, let us prove") that appears also in Volpone.

Jonson set out in 1618 for his ancestral Scotland on foot. He spent over a year there, and the best-remembered hospitality which he enjoyed was that of the Scottish poet, William Drummond of Hawthornden, in April 1619, sited on the River Esk. Drummond undertook to record as much of Jonson's conversation as he could in his diary, and thus recorded aspects of Jonson's personality that might otherwise have been lost. Jonson delivers his opinions, in Drummond's terse reporting, in an expansive and even magisterial mood. Drummond noted he was "a great lover and praiser of himself, a contemner and scorner of others".

In Edinburgh he was made an honorary citizen of Edinburgh.

From there he travelled west and lodged with the Duke of Lennox where he wrote a play based on Loch Lomond.

On returning to England, he was awarded an honorary Master of Arts degree from Oxford University.

Jonson's creativity began to decline in the 1620s. He was still well-known and many looked up to him as both mentor and for guidance. These were called the "Sons of Ben" or the "Tribe of Ben", in their number were poets such as Robert Herrick, Richard Lovelace, and Sir John Suckling who took their bearing in verse from Jonson. Though his strength and reputation were waning he did resume writing regular plays. Although these failed to emulate his former gems they do have interesting angles, especially of Charles I. The Staple of News also offers a remarkable look at the earliest stage of English journalism.

In 1623, historian Edmund Bolton named him the best and most polished English poet. That this judgment was widely shared is indicated by the admitted influence he had on younger poets. The grounds for describing Jonson as the "father" of cavalier poets are clear: as noted previously, many of the cavalier poets described themselves as his "sons" or his "tribe". For some of them, the connection was as much social as poetic; Herrick described meetings at "the Sun, the Dog, the Triple Tunne". All of them, including those like Herrick whose accomplishments in verse are generally regarded as superior to Jonson's, took inspiration from Jonson's revival of classical forms and themes, his subtle melodies, and his disciplined use of wit. In these respects Jonson may be regarded as among the most important figures in the history of English neoclassicism.

The principal factor in Jonson's partial eclipse was the death of James and the accession of King Charles I in 1625. Jonson felt neglected by the new court. A decisive quarrel with Jones harmed his career as a writer of court masques, although he continued to entertain the court on an irregular basis. For his part, Charles displayed a certain affection for the great poet of his father's day: he therefore increased Jonson's annual pension to £100 and included a tierce of wine.

Family tragedy struck again in 1635 when a second son, also named Benjamin Jonson, died. In that period, Ann Lewis and Ben Jonson lived separate lives for several years; their martial arrangement cast Ann Lewis as the housewife Jonson, and Ben Jonson as the artist who enjoyed the residential hospitality of his patrons, Sir Robert Townshend and Lord Aubigny, Esme Stuart, 3rd Duke of Lennox.

Ben Jonson died on August 6th, 1637. At his death he seems to have been working on another play, The Sad Shepherd. Though only two acts are extant, this represents a remarkable new direction for Jonson: a move into pastoral drama.

His funeral was held on August 9th. He is buried in the north aisle of the nave in Westminster Abbey, with the inscription "O Rare Ben Johnson" set in the slab over his grave.

The fact that Jonson was buried in an upright position was either an indication of his reduced circumstances at the time of his death, or, alternatively it has been written that he asked for a grave exactly 18 inches square from the monarch and received an upright grave to fit in the requested space.

There is a suggestion that the inscription could be read "Orare Ben Jonson" (pray for Ben Jonson), which would fit on many religious levels on the soul but the carving shows a distinct space between "O" and "rare".

In 1723 a monument to Jonson was erected by the Earl of Oxford and is in the eastern aisle of Westminster Abbey's Poets' Corner. It includes a portrait medallion and the same inscription as on the gravestone. It seems Jonson was to have had a monument erected by subscription soon after his death but with the advent of the English Civil War this did not happen.

In summing up Ben Jonson was a classically educated, well-read, and cultured man of the English Renaissance with a large appetite for controversy (personal and political, artistic and intellectual) whose cultural influence was of unparalleled breadth upon the playwrights and the poets of the Jacobean era (1603–1625) and of the Caroline era (1625–1642).

During the 17th century Jonson was a towering literary figure, and he has been described as 'One of the most vigorous minds that ever added to the strength of English literature'. Before the English Civil War, the "Tribe of Ben" touted his importance, and during the Restoration Jonson's satirical comedies and his theory and practice of "humour characters" was extremely influential, providing the model for many Restoration comedies.

In the 18th century Jonson's status began to decline and by the Romantic era, Jonson suffered the fate of being unfairly compared and contrasted to Shakespeare. It is only now, hundred of years later that his true worth can be assessed and he can be placed in the very front rank of English literary figures.

Ben Jonson – A Concise Bibliography

Plays

A Tale of a Tub, comedy (c. 1596 revised, performed 1633)
The Isle of Dogs, comedy (1597, with Thomas Nashe)
The Case is Altered, comedy (c. 1597–98), with Henry Porter and Anthony Munday
Every Man in His Humour, comedy (performed 1598)
Every Man out of His Humour, comedy (performed 1599)
Cynthia's Revels (performed 1600)
The Poetaster, comedy (performed 1601)
Sejanus His Fall, tragedy (performed 1603)
Eastward Ho, comedy (performed 1605), a collaboration with John Marston and George Chapman
Volpone, comedy (c. 1605–06)
Epicoene, or the Silent Woman, comedy (performed)
The Alchemist, comedy (performed 1610)
Catiline His Conspiracy, tragedy (performed 1611)
Bartholomew Fair, comedy (performed 31 October 1614)
The Devil is an Ass, comedy (performed 1616)
The Staple of News, comedy (performed February 1626)
The New Inn, or The Light Heart, comedy (licensed 19 January 1629)
The Magnetic Lady, or Humors Reconciled, comedy (licensed 12 October 1632)
The Sad Shepherd, pastoral (c. 1637), unfinished
Mortimer His Fall, history (printed 1641), a fragment

Masques

The Coronation Triumph, or The King's Entertainment (performed 15 March 1604) with Thomas Dekker
A Private Entertainment of the King and Queen on May-Day (The Penates) (1 May 1604)
The Entertainment of the Queen and Prince Henry at Althorp (The Satyr) (25 June 1603)
The Masque of Blackness (6 January 1605)
Hymenaei (5 January 1606)
The Entertainment of the Kings of Great Britain and Denmark (The Hours) (24 July 1606)

The Masque of Beauty (10 January 1608)
The Masque of Queens (2 February 1609)
The Hue and Cry After Cupid, or The Masque at Lord Haddington's Marriage (9 February 1608)
The Entertainment at Britain's Burse (11 April 1609)
The Speeches at Prince Henry's Barriers, or The Lady of the Lake (6 January 1610)
Oberon, the Faery Prince (1 January 1611)
Love Freed from Ignorance and Folly (3 February 1611)
Love Restored (6 January 1612)
A Challenge at Tilt, at a Marriage (27 December 1613/1 January 1614)
The Irish Masque at Court (29 December 1613)
Mercury Vindicated from the Alchemists (6 January 1615)
The Golden Age Restored (1 January 1616)
Christmas, His Masque (Christmas 1616)
The Vision of Delight (6 January 1617)
Lovers Made Men, or The Masque of Lethe, or The Masque at Lord Hay's (22 February 1617)
Pleasure Reconciled to Virtue (6 January 1618) The masque was a failure; Jonson revised it by placing the anti-masque first, turning it into:-
For the Honour of Wales (17 February 1618)
News from the New World Discovered in the Moon (7 January 1620)
The Entertainment at Blackfriars, or The Newcastle Entertainment (May 1620)
Pan's Anniversary, or The Shepherd's Holy-Day (19 June 1620)
The Gypsies Metamorphosed (3 and 5 August 1621)
The Masque of Augurs (6 January 1622)
Time Vindicated to Himself and to His Honours (19 January 1623)
Neptune's Triumph for the Return of Albion (26 January 1624)
The Masque of Owls at Kenilworth (19 August 1624)
The Fortunate Isles and Their Union (9 January 1625)
Love's Triumph Through Callipolis (9 January 1631)
Chloridia: Rites to Chloris and Her Nymphs (22 February 1631)
The King's Entertainment at Welbeck in Nottinghamshire (21 May 1633)
Love's Welcome at Bolsover (30 July 1634)

Other Works
Epigrams (1612)
The Forest (1616), including To Penshurst
On My First Sonne (1616), elegy
A Discourse of Love (1618)
Barclay's Argenis, translated by Jonson (1623)
The Execration against Vulcan (1640)
Horace's Art of Poetry, translated by Jonson (1640)
Underwood (1640)
English Grammar (1640)
Timber, or Discoveries made upon men and matter, as they have flowed out of his daily readings, or had their reflux to his peculiar notion of the times, a commonplace book
To Celia (Drink to Me Only With Thine Eyes), poem

The greatest of English dramatists except Shakespeare, the first literary dictator and poet-laureate, a writer of verse, prose, satire, and criticism who most potently of all the men of his time affected the subsequent course of English letters: such was Ben Jonson, and as such his strong personality assumes an interest to us almost unparalleled, at least in his age.

Ben Jonson came of the stock that was centuries after to give to the world Thomas Carlyle; for Jonson's grandfather was of Annandale, over the Solway, whence he migrated to England. Jonson's father lost his estate under Queen Mary, "having been cast into prison and forfeited." He entered the church, but died a month before his illustrious son was born, leaving his widow and child in poverty. Jonson's birthplace was Westminster, and the time of his birth early in 1573. He was thus nearly ten years Shakespeare's junior, and less well off, if a trifle better born. But Jonson did not profit even by this slight advantage. His mother married beneath her, a wright or bricklayer, and Jonson was for a time apprenticed to the trade. As a youth he attracted the attention of the famous antiquary, William Camden, then usher at Westminster School, and there the poet laid the solid foundations of his classical learning. Jonson always held Camden in veneration, acknowledging that to him he owed,

"All that I am in arts, all that I know;"

and dedicating his first dramatic success, "Every Man in His Humour," to him. It is doubtful whether Jonson ever went to either university, though Fuller says that he was "statutably admitted into St. John's College, Cambridge." He tells us that he took no degree, but was later "Master of Arts in both the universities, by their favour, not his study." When a mere youth Jonson enlisted as a soldier, trailing his pike in Flanders in the protracted wars of William the Silent against the Spanish. Jonson was a large and raw-boned lad; he became by his own account in time exceedingly bulky. In chat with his friend William Drummond of Hawthornden, Jonson told how "in his service in the Low Countries he had, in the face of both the camps, killed an enemy, and taken opima spolia from him;" and how "since his coming to England, being appealed to the fields, he had killed his adversary which had hurt him in the arm and whose sword was ten inches longer than his." Jonson's reach may have made up for the lack of his sword; certainly his prowess lost nothing in the telling. Obviously Jonson was brave, combative, and not averse to talking of himself and his doings.

In 1592, Jonson returned from abroad penniless. Soon after he married, almost as early and quite as imprudently as Shakespeare. He told Drummond curtly that "his wife was a shrew, yet honest"; for some years he lived apart from her in the household of Lord Albany. Yet two touching epitaphs among Jonson's "Epigrams," "On my first daughter," and "On my first son," attest the warmth of the poet's family affections. The daughter died in infancy, the son of the plague; another son grew up to manhood little credit to his father whom he survived. We know nothing beyond this of Jonson's domestic life.

How soon Jonson drifted into what we now call grandly "the theatrical profession" we do not know. In 1593, Marlowe made his tragic exit from life, and Greene, Shakespeare's other rival on the popular stage, had preceded Marlowe in an equally miserable death the year before. Shakespeare already had the running to himself. Jonson appears first in the employment of Philip Henslowe, the exploiter of several troupes of players, manager, and father-in-law of the famous actor, Edward Alleyn. From entries in "Henslowe's Diary," a species of theatrical account book which has been handed down to us, we know that Jonson was connected with the Admiral's men; for he borrowed 4 pounds of Henslowe, July 28, 1597, paying back 3s. 9d. on the same day on account of his "share" (in what is not altogether clear); while later, on December 3, of the same year, Henslowe advanced 20s. to him "upon a book which he showed the plot unto the company which he promised to deliver unto the company at Christmas next." In the next August Jonson was in collaboration with Chettle and

Porter in a play called "Hot Anger Soon Cold." All this points to an association with Henslowe of some duration, as no mere tyro would be thus paid in advance upon mere promise. From allusions in Dekker's play, "Satiromastix," it appears that Jonson, like Shakespeare, began life as an actor, and that he "ambled in a leather pitch by a play-wagon" taking at one time the part of Hieronimo in Kyd's famous play, "The Spanish Tragedy." By the beginning of 1598, Jonson, though still in needy circumstances, had begun to receive recognition. Francis Meres -- well known for his "Comparative Discourse of our English Poets with the Greek, Latin, and Italian Poets," printed in 1598, and for his mention therein of a dozen plays of Shakespeare by title -- accords to Ben Jonson a place as one of "our best in tragedy," a matter of some surprise, as no known tragedy of Jonson from so early a date has come down to us. That Jonson was at work on tragedy, however, is proved by the entries in Henslowe of at least three tragedies, now lost, in which he had a hand. These are "Page of Plymouth," "King Robert II. of Scotland," and "Richard Crookback." But all of these came later, on his return to Henslowe, and range from August 1599 to June 1602.

Returning to the autumn of 1598, an event now happened to sever for a time Jonson's relations with Henslowe. In a letter to Alleyn, dated September 26 of that year, Henslowe writes: "I have lost one of my company that hurteth me greatly; that is Gabriel [Spencer], for he is slain in Hogsden fields by the hands of Benjamin Jonson, bricklayer." The last word is perhaps Henslowe's thrust at Jonson in his displeasure rather than a designation of his actual continuance at his trade up to this time. It is fair to Jonson to remark however, that his adversary appears to have been a notorious fire-eater who had shortly before killed one Feeke in a similar squabble. Duelling was a frequent occurrence of the time among gentlemen and the nobility; it was an impudent breach of the peace on the part of a player. This duel is the one which Jonson described years after to Drummond, and for it Jonson was duly arraigned at Old Bailey, tried, and convicted. He was sent to prison and such goods and chattels as he had "were forfeited." It is a thought to give one pause that, but for the ancient law permitting convicted felons to plead, as it was called, the benefit of clergy, Jonson might have been hanged for this deed. The circumstance that the poet could read and write saved him; and he received only a brand of the letter "T," for Tyburn, on his left thumb. While in jail Jonson became a Roman Catholic; but he returned to the faith of the Church of England a dozen years later.

On his release, in disgrace with Henslowe and his former associates, Jonson offered his services as a playwright to Henslowe's rivals, the Lord Chamberlain's company, in which Shakespeare was a prominent shareholder. A tradition of long standing, though not susceptible of proof in a court of law, narrates that Jonson had submitted the manuscript of "Every Man in His Humour" to the Chamberlain's men and had received from the company a refusal; that Shakespeare called him back, read the play himself, and at once accepted it. Whether this story is true or not, certain it is that "Every Man in His Humour" was accepted by Shakespeare's company and acted for the first time in 1598, with Shakespeare taking a part. The evidence of this is contained in the list of actors prefixed to the comedy in the folio of Jonson's works, 1616. But it is a mistake to infer, because Shakespeare's name stands first in the list of actors and the elder Kno'well first in the dramatis personae, that Shakespeare took that particular part. The order of a list of Elizabethan players was generally that of their importance or priority as shareholders in the company and seldom if ever corresponded to the list of characters.

"Every Man in His Humour" was an immediate success, and with it Jonson's reputation as one of the leading dramatists of his time was established once and for all. This could have been by no means Jonson's earliest comedy, and we have just learned that he was already reputed one of "our best in tragedy." Indeed, one of Jonson's extant comedies, "The Case is Altered," but one never claimed by him or published as his, must certainly have preceded "Every Man in His Humour" on the stage. The former play may be described as a comedy modelled on the Latin plays of Plautus. (It combines, in fact, situations derived from the "Captivi" and the "Aulularia" of that dramatist). But the pretty story of the beggar-maiden, Rachel, and her suitors, Jonson found, not among the classics, but in the ideals of romantic love which Shakespeare had already popularised on the stage. Jonson never again produced so fresh and lovable a feminine personage as Rachel, although in other respects "The Case is Altered" is not a conspicuous play, and, save for the satirising of Antony Munday in the person of Antonio Balladino and Gabriel Harvey as well, is perhaps the least characteristic of the comedies of Jonson.

"Every Man in His Humour," probably first acted late in the summer of 1598 and at the Curtain, is commonly regarded as an epoch-making play; and this view is not unjustified. As to plot, it tells little more than how an intercepted letter enabled a father to follow his supposedly studious son to London, and there observe his life with the gallants of the time. The real quality of this comedy is in its personages and in the theory upon which they are conceived. Ben Jonson had theories about poetry and the drama, and he was neither chary in talking of them nor in experimenting with them in his plays. This makes Jonson, like Dryden in his time, and Wordsworth much later, an author to reckon with; particularly when we remember that many of Jonson's notions came for a time definitely to prevail and to modify the whole trend of English poetry. First of all Jonson was a classicist, that is, he believed in restraint and precedent in art in opposition to the prevalent ungoverned and irresponsible Renaissance spirit. Jonson believed that there was a professional way of doing things which might be reached by a study of the best examples, and he found these examples for the most part among the ancients. To confine our attention to the drama, Jonson objected to the amateurishness and haphazard nature of many contemporary plays, and set himself to do something different; and the first and most striking thing that he evolved was his conception and practice of the comedy of humours.

As Jonson has been much misrepresented in this matter, let us quote his own words as to "humour." A humour, according to Jonson, was a bias of disposition, a warp, so to speak, in character by which

"Some one peculiar quality
Doth so possess a man, that it doth draw
All his affects, his spirits, and his powers,
In their confluctions, all to run one way."

But continuing, Jonson is careful to add:

"But that a rook by wearing a pied feather,
The cable hat-band, or the three-piled ruff,
A yard of shoe-tie, or the Switzers knot
On his French garters, should affect a humour!
O, it is more than most ridiculous."

Jonson's comedy of humours, in a word, conceived of stage personages on the basis of a ruling trait or passion (a notable simplification of actual life be it observed in passing); and, placing these typified traits in juxtaposition in their conflict and contrast, struck the spark of comedy. Downright, as his name indicates, is "a plain squire"; Bobadill's humour is that of the braggart who is incidentally, and with delightfully comic effect, a coward; Brainworm's humour is the finding out of things to the end of fooling everybody: of course he is fooled in the end himself. But it was not Jonson's theories alone that made the success of "Every Man in His Humour." The play is admirably written and each character is vividly conceived, and with a firm touch based on observation of the men of the London of the day. Jonson was neither in this, his first great comedy (nor in any other play that he wrote), a supine classicist, urging that English drama return to a slavish adherence to classical conditions. He says as to the laws of the old comedy (meaning by "laws," such matters as the unities of time and place and the use of chorus): "I see not then, but we should enjoy the same licence, or free power to illustrate and heighten our invention as they [the ancients] did; and not be tied to those strict and regular forms which the niceness of a few, who are nothing but form, would thrust upon us." "Every Man in His Humour" is written in prose, a novel practice which Jonson had of his predecessor in comedy, John Lyly. Even the word "humour" seems to have been employed in the Jonsonian sense by Chapman before Jonson's use of it. Indeed, the comedy of humours itself is only a heightened variety of the comedy of manners which represents life, viewed at a satirical angle, and is the oldest and most persistent species of comedy in the language. None the less, Jonson's comedy merited its immediate success and marked out a definite course in which comedy long continued to run. To mention only Shakespeare's Falstaff and his rout, Bardolph, Pistol, Dame Quickly, and the rest, whether in "Henry IV." or in "The Merry Wives of Windsor," all are conceived in the spirit of humours. So are the captains, Welsh, Scotch, and Irish of "Henry V.," and Malvolio especially later; though Shakespeare never employed the method of humours for an important personage. It was not Jonson's fault that many of his successors did precisely the thing that he had reprobated, that is, degrade the humour: into an oddity of speech, an eccentricity of manner, of dress, or cut of beard. There was an anonymous play called "Every Woman in Her Humour." Chapman wrote "A Humourous Day's Mirth," Day, "Humour Out of Breath," Fletcher later, "The Humourous Lieutenant," and Jonson, besides "Every Man Out of His Humour," returned to the title in closing the cycle of his comedies in "The Magnetic Lady or Humours Reconciled."

With the performance of "Every Man Out of His Humour" in 1599, by Shakespeare's company once more at the Globe, we turn a new page in Jonson's career. Despite his many real virtues, if there is one feature more than any other that distinguishes Jonson, it is his arrogance; and to this may be added his self-righteousness, especially under criticism or satire. "Every Man Out of His Humour" is the first of three "comical satires" which Jonson contributed to what Dekker called the poetomachia or war of the theatres as recent critics have named it. This play as a fabric of plot is a very slight affair; but as a satirical picture of the manners of the time, proceeding by means of vivid caricature, couched in witty and brilliant dialogue and sustained by that righteous indignation which must lie at the heart of all true satire -- as a realisation, in short, of the classical ideal of comedy -- there had been nothing like Jonson's comedy since the days of Aristophanes. "Every Man in His Humour," like the two plays that follow it, contains two kinds of attack, the critical or generally satiric, levelled at abuses and corruptions in the abstract; and the personal, in which specific application is made of all this in the lampooning of poets and others, Jonson's contemporaries. The method of personal attack by actual caricature of a person on the stage is almost as old as the drama. Aristophanes so lampooned Euripides in "The Acharnians" and Socrates in "The Clouds," to mention no other examples; and in English drama this kind of thing is alluded to again and again. What Jonson really did, was to raise the dramatic lampoon to an art, and make out of a casual burlesque and bit of mimicry a dramatic satire of literary pretensions and permanency. With the arrogant attitude mentioned above and his uncommon eloquence in scorn, vituperation, and invective, it is no wonder that Jonson soon involved himself in literary and even personal quarrels with his fellow-authors. The circumstances of the origin of this 'poetomachia' are far from clear, and those who have written on the topic, except of late, have not helped to make them clearer. The origin of the "war" has been referred to satirical references, apparently to Jonson, contained in "The Scourge of Villainy," a satire in regular form after the manner of the ancients by John Marston, a fellow playwright, subsequent friend and collaborator of Jonson's. On the other hand, epigrams of Jonson have been discovered (49, 68, and 100) variously charging "playwright" (reasonably identified with Marston) with scurrility, cowardice, and plagiarism; though the dates of the epigrams cannot be ascertained with certainty. Jonson's own statement of the matter to Drummond runs: "He had many quarrels with Marston, beat him, and took his pistol from him, wrote his "Poetaster" on him; the beginning[s] of them were that Marston represented him on the stage."*

*The best account of this whole subject is to be found in the edition of "Poetaster" and "Satiromastrix" by J. H. Penniman in "Belles Lettres Series" shortly to appear. See also his earlier work, "The War of the Theatres," 1892, and the excellent contributions to the subject by H. C. Hart in "Notes and Queries," and in his edition of Jonson, 1906.

Here at least we are on certain ground; and the principals of the quarrel are known. "Histriomastix," a play revised by Marston in 1598, has been regarded as the one in which Jonson was thus "represented on the stage"; although the personage in question, Chrisogonus, a poet, satirist, and translator, poor but proud, and contemptuous of the common herd, seems rather a complimentary portrait of Jonson than a caricature. As to the personages actually ridiculed in "Every Man Out of His Humour," Carlo Buffone was formerly thought certainly to be Marston, as he was described as "a public, scurrilous, and profane jester," and elsewhere as the grand scourge or second untruss [that is, satirist], of the time (Joseph Hall being by his own boast the first, and Marston's work being entitled "The Scourge of Villainy"). Apparently we must now prefer for Carlo a notorious character named Charles Chester, of whom gossipy and inaccurate Aubrey relates that he was "a bold impertinent fellow...a perpetual talker and made a noise like a drum in a room. So one time at a tavern Sir Walter Raleigh beats him and seals up his mouth (that is his upper and nether beard) with hard wax. From him Ben Jonson takes his Carlo Buffone ['i.e.', jester] in "Every Man in His Humour" ['sic']." Is it conceivable that after all Jonson was ridiculing Marston, and that the point of the satire consisted in an intentional confusion of "the grand scourge or second untruss" with "the scurrilous and profane" Chester?

We have digressed into detail in this particular case to exemplify the difficulties of criticism in its attempts to identify the allusions in these forgotten quarrels. We are on sounder ground of fact in recording other manifestations of Jonson's enmity. In "The Case is Altered" there is clear ridicule in the character Antonio Balladino of Anthony Munday, pageant-poet of the city, translator of romances and playwright as well. In "Every Man in His Humour" there is certainly a caricature of Samuel Daniel, accepted poet of the court, sonneteer, and companion of men of fashion. These men held recognised positions to which Jonson felt his talents better entitled him; they were hence to him his natural enemies. It seems almost certain that he pursued both in the personages of his satire through "Every Man Out of His Humour," and "Cynthia's Revels," Daniel under the characters Fastidious Brisk and Hedon, Munday as Puntarvolo and Amorphus; but in these last we venture on quagmire once more. Jonson's literary rivalry of Daniel is traceable again and again, in the entertainments that welcomed King James on his way to London, in the masques at court, and in the pastoral drama. As to Jonson's personal ambitions with respect to these two men, it is notable that he became, not pageant-poet, but chronologer to the City of London; and that, on the accession of the new king, he came soon to triumph over Daniel as the accepted entertainer of royalty.

"Cynthia's Revels," the second "comical satire," was acted in 1600, and, as a play, is even more lengthy, elaborate, and impossible than "Every Man Out of His Humour." Here personal satire seems to have absorbed everything, and while much of the caricature is admirable, especially in the detail of witty and trenchantly satirical dialogue, the central idea of a fountain of self-love is not very well carried out, and the persons revert at times to abstractions, the action to allegory. It adds to our wonder that this difficult drama should have been acted by the Children of Queen Elizabeth's Chapel, among them Nathaniel Field with whom Jonson read Horace and Martial, and whom he taught later how to make plays. Another of these precocious little actors was Salathiel Pavy, who died before he was thirteen, already famed for taking the parts of old men. Him Jonson immortalised in one of the sweetest of his epitaphs. An interesting sidelight is this on the character of this redoubtable and rugged satirist, that he should thus have befriended and tenderly remembered these little theatrical waifs, some of whom (as we know) had been literally kidnapped to be pressed into the service of the theatre and whipped to the conning of their difficult parts. To the caricature of Daniel and Munday in "Cynthia's Revels" must be added Anaides (impudence), here assuredly Marston, and Asotus (the prodigal), interpreted as Lodge or, more perilously, Raleigh. Crites, like Asper-Macilente in "Every Man Out of His Humour," is Jonson's self-complaisant portrait of himself, the just, wholly admirable, and judicious scholar, holding his head high above the pack of the yelping curs of envy and detraction, but careless of their puny attacks on his perfections with only too mindful a neglect.

The third and last of the "comical satires" is "Poetaster," acted, once more, by the Children of the Chapel in 1601, and Jonson's only avowed contribution to the fray. According to the author's own account, this play was written in fifteen weeks on a report that his enemies had entrusted to Dekker the preparation of "Satiromastix, the Untrussing of the Humorous Poet," a dramatic attack upon himself. In this attempt to forestall his enemies Jonson succeeded, and "Poetaster" was an immediate and deserved success. While hardly more closely knit in structure than its earlier companion pieces, "Poetaster" is planned to lead up to the ludicrous final scene in which, after a device borrowed from the "Lexiphanes" of Lucian, the offending poetaster, Marston-Crispinus, is made to throw up the difficult words with which he had overburdened his stomach as well as overlarded his vocabulary. In the end Crispinus with his fellow, Dekker-Demetrius, is bound over to keep the peace and never thenceforward "malign, traduce, or detract the person or writings of Quintus Horatius Flaccus [Jonson] or any other eminent man transcending you in merit." One of the most diverting personages in Jonson's comedy is Captain Tucca. "His peculiarity" has been well described by Ward as "a buoyant blackguardism which recovers itself instantaneously from the most complete exposure, and a picturesqueness of speech like that of a walking dictionary of slang."

It was this character, Captain Tucca, that Dekker hit upon in his reply, "Satiromastix," and he amplified him, turning his abusive vocabulary back upon Jonson and adding "an immodesty to his dialogue that did not enter into Jonson's conception." It has been held, altogether plausibly, that when Dekker was engaged professionally, so to speak, to write a dramatic reply to Jonson, he was at work on a species of chronicle history, dealing with the story of Walter Terill in the reign of William Rufus. This he hurriedly adapted to include the satirical characters suggested by "Poetaster," and fashioned to convey the satire of his reply. The absurdity of placing Horace in the court of a Norman king is the result. But Dekker's play is not without its palpable hits at the arrogance, the literary pride, and self-righteousness of Jonson-Horace, whose "ningle" or pal, the absurd Asinius Bubo, has recently been shown to figure forth, in all likelihood, Jonson's friend, the poet Drayton. Slight and hastily adapted as is "Satiromastix," especially in a comparison with the better wrought and more significant satire of "Poetaster," the town awarded the palm to Dekker, not to Jonson; and Jonson gave over in consequence his practice of "comical satire." Though Jonson was cited to appear before the Lord Chief Justice to answer certain charges to the effect that he had attacked lawyers and soldiers in "Poetaster," nothing came of this complaint. It may be suspected that much of this furious clatter and give-and-take was pure playing to the gallery. The town was agog with the strife, and on no less an authority than Shakespeare ("Hamlet," ii. 2), we learn that the children's company (acting the plays of Jonson) did "so berattle the common stages...that many, wearing rapiers, are afraid of goose-quills, and dare scarce come thither."

Several other plays have been thought to bear a greater or less part in the war of the theatres. Among them the most important is a college play, entitled "The Return from Parnassus," dating 1601-02. In it a much-quoted passage makes Burbage, as a character, declare: "Why here's our fellow Shakespeare puts them all down; aye and Ben Jonson, too. O that Ben Jonson is a pestilent fellow; he brought up Horace, giving the poets a pill, but our fellow Shakespeare hath given him a purge that made him bewray his credit." Was Shakespeare then concerned in this war of the stages? And what could have been the nature of this "purge"? Among several suggestions, "Troilus and Cressida" has been thought by some to be the play in which Shakespeare thus "put down" his friend,

Jonson. A wiser interpretation finds the "purge" in "Satiromastix," which, though not written by Shakespeare, was staged by his company, and therefore with his approval and under his direction as one of the leaders of that company.

The last years of the reign of Elizabeth thus saw Jonson recognised as a dramatist second only to Shakespeare, and not second even to him as a dramatic satirist. But Jonson now turned his talents to new fields. Plays on subjects derived from classical story and myth had held the stage from the beginning of the drama, so that Shakespeare was making no new departure when he wrote his "Julius Caesar" about 1600. Therefore when Jonson staged "Sejanus," three years later and with Shakespeare's company once more, he was only following in the elder dramatist's footsteps. But Jonson's idea of a play on classical history, on the one hand, and Shakespeare's and the elder popular dramatists, on the other, were very different. Heywood some years before had put five straggling plays on the stage in quick succession, all derived from stories in Ovid and dramatised with little taste or discrimination. Shakespeare had a finer conception of form, but even he was contented to take all his ancient history from North's translation of Plutarch and dramatise his subject without further inquiry. Jonson was a scholar and a classical antiquarian. He reprobated this slipshod amateurishness, and wrote his "Sejanus" like a scholar, reading Tacitus, Suetonius, and other authorities, to be certain of his facts, his setting, and his atmosphere, and somewhat pedantically noting his authorities in the margin when he came to print. "Sejanus" is a tragedy of genuine dramatic power in which is told with discriminating taste the story of the haughty favourite of Tiberius with his tragical overthrow. Our drama presents no truer nor more painstaking representation of ancient Roman life than may be found in Jonson's "Sejanus" and "Catiline his Conspiracy," which followed in 1611. A passage in the address of the former play to the reader, in which Jonson refers to a collaboration in an earlier version, has led to the surmise that Shakespeare may have been that "worthier pen." There is no evidence to determine the matter.

In 1605, we find Jonson in active collaboration with Chapman and Marston in the admirable comedy of London life entitled "Eastward Hoe." In the previous year, Marston had dedicated his "Malcontent," in terms of fervid admiration, to Jonson; so that the wounds of the war of the theatres must have been long since healed. Between Jonson and Chapman there was the kinship of similar scholarly ideals. The two continued friends throughout life. "Eastward Hoe" achieved the extraordinary popularity represented in a demand for three issues in one year. But this was not due entirely to the merits of the play. In its earliest version a passage which an irritable courtier conceived to be derogatory to his nation, the Scots, sent both Chapman and Jonson to jail; but the matter was soon patched up, for by this time Jonson had influence at court.

With the accession of King James, Jonson began his long and successful career as a writer of masques. He wrote more masques than all his competitors together, and they are of an extraordinary variety and poetic excellence. Jonson did not invent the masque; for such premeditated devices to set and frame, so to speak, a court ball had been known and practised in varying degrees of elaboration long before his time. But Jonson gave dramatic value to the masque, especially in his invention of the antimasque, a comedy or farcical element of relief, entrusted to professional players or dancers. He enhanced, as well, the beauty and dignity of those portions of the masque in which noble lords and ladies took their parts to create, by their gorgeous costumes and artistic grouping and evolutions, a sumptuous show. On the mechanical and scenic side Jonson had an inventive and ingenious partner in Inigo Jones, the royal architect, who more than any one man raised the standard of stage representation in the England of his day. Jonson continued active in the service of the court in the writing of masques and other entertainments far into the reign of King Charles; but, towards the end, a quarrel with Jones embittered his life, and the two testy old men appear to have become not only a constant irritation to each other, but intolerable bores at court. In "Hymenaei," "The Masque of Queens," "Love Freed from Ignorance," "Lovers made Men,"

"Pleasure Reconciled to Virtue," and many more will be found Jonson's aptitude, his taste, his poetry and inventiveness in these by-forms of the drama; while in "The Masque of Christmas," and "The Gipsies Metamorphosed" especially, is discoverable that power of broad comedy which, at court as well as in the city, was not the least element of Jonson's contemporary popularity.

But Jonson had by no means given up the popular stage when he turned to the amusement of King James. In 1605 "Volpone" was produced, "The Silent Woman" in 1609, "The Alchemist" in the following year. These comedies, with "Bartholomew Fair," 1614, represent Jonson at his height, and for constructive cleverness, character successfully conceived in the manner of caricature, wit and brilliancy of dialogue, they stand alone in English drama. "Volpone, or the Fox," is, in a sense, a transition play from the dramatic satires of the war of the theatres to the purer comedy represented in the plays named above. Its subject is a struggle of wit applied to chicanery; for among its dramatis personae, from the villainous Fox himself, his rascally servant Mosca, Voltore (the vulture), Corbaccio and Corvino (the big and the little raven), to Sir Politic Would-be and the rest, there is scarcely a virtuous character in the play. Question has been raised as to whether a story so forbidding can be considered a comedy, for, although the plot ends in the discomfiture and imprisonment of the most vicious, it involves no mortal catastrophe. But Jonson was on sound historical ground, for "Volpone" is conceived far more logically on the lines of the ancients' theory of comedy than was ever the romantic drama of Shakespeare, however repulsive we may find a philosophy of life that facilely divides the world into the rogues and their dupes, and, identifying brains with roguery and innocence with folly, admires the former while inconsistently punishing them.

"The Silent Woman" is a gigantic farce of the most ingenious construction. The whole comedy hinges on a huge joke, played by a heartless nephew on his misanthropic uncle, who is induced to take to himself a wife, young, fair, and warranted silent, but who, in the end, turns out neither silent nor a woman at all. In "The Alchemist," again, we have the utmost cleverness in construction, the whole fabric building climax on climax, witty, ingenious, and so plausibly presented that we forget its departures from the possibilities of life. In "The Alchemist" Jonson represented, none the less to the life, certain sharpers of the metropolis, revelling in their shrewdness and rascality and in the variety of the stupidity and wickedness of their victims. We may object to the fact that the only person in the play possessed of a scruple of honesty is discomfited, and that the greatest scoundrel of all is approved in the end and rewarded. The comedy is so admirably written and contrived, the personages stand out with such lifelike distinctness in their several kinds, and the whole is animated with such verve and resourcefulness that "The Alchemist" is a new marvel every time it is read. Lastly of this group comes the tremendous comedy, "Bartholomew Fair," less clear cut, less definite, and less structurally worthy of praise than its three predecessors, but full of the keenest and cleverest of satire and inventive to a degree beyond any English comedy save some other of Jonson's own. It is in "Bartholomew Fair" that we are presented to the immortal caricature of the Puritan, Zeal-in-the-Land Busy, and the Littlewits that group about him, and it is in this extraordinary comedy that the humour of Jonson, always open to this danger, loosens into the Rabelaisian mode that so delighted King James in "The Gipsies Metamorphosed." Another comedy of less merit is "The Devil is an Ass," acted in 1616. It was the failure of this play that caused Jonson to give over writing for the public stage for a period of nearly ten years.

"Volpone" was laid as to scene in Venice. Whether because of the success of "Eastward Hoe" or for other reasons, the other three comedies declare in the words of the prologue to "The Alchemist":

"Our scene is London, 'cause we would make known No country's mirth is better than our own."

Indeed Jonson went further when he came to revise his plays for collected publication in his folio of 1616, he transferred the scene of "Every Man in His Humour" from Florence to London also, converting Signior Lorenzo di Pazzi to Old Kno'well, Prospero to Master Welborn, and Hesperida to Dame Kitely "dwelling i' the Old Jewry."

In his comedies of London life, despite his trend towards caricature, Jonson has shown himself a genuine realist, drawing from the life about him with an experience and insight rare in any generation. A happy comparison has been suggested between Ben Jonson and Charles Dickens. Both were men of the people, lowly born and hardly bred. Each knew the London of his time as few men knew it; and each represented it intimately and in elaborate detail. Both men were at heart moralists, seeking the truth by the exaggerated methods of humour and caricature; perverse, even wrong-headed at times, but possessed of a true pathos and largeness of heart, and when all has been said -- though the Elizabethan ran to satire, the Victorian to sentimentality -- leaving the world better for the art that they practised in it.

In 1616, the year of the death of Shakespeare, Jonson collected his plays, his poetry, and his masques for publication in a collective edition. This was an unusual thing at the time and had been attempted by no dramatist before Jonson. This volume published, in a carefully revised text, all the plays thus far mentioned, excepting "The Case is Altered," which Jonson did not acknowledge, "Bartholomew Fair," and "The Devil is an Ass," which was written too late. It included likewise a book of some hundred and thirty odd "Epigrams," in which form of brief and pungent writing Jonson was an acknowledged master; "The Forest," a smaller collection of lyric and occasional verse and some ten "Masques" and "Entertainments." In this same year Jonson was made poet laureate with a pension of one hundred marks a year. This, with his fees and returns from several noblemen, and the small earnings of his plays must have formed the bulk of his income. The poet appears to have done certain literary hack-work for others, as, for example, parts of the Punic Wars contributed to Raleigh's "History of the World." We know from a story, little to the credit of either, that Jonson accompanied Raleigh's son abroad in the capacity of a tutor. In 1618 Jonson was granted the reversion of the office of Master of the Revels, a post for which he was peculiarly fitted; but he did not live to enjoy its perquisites. Jonson was honoured with degrees by both universities, though when and under what circumstances is not known. It has been said that he narrowly escaped the honour of knighthood, which the satirists of the day averred King James was wont to lavish with an indiscriminate hand. Worse men were made knights in his day than worthy Ben Jonson.

From 1616 to the close of the reign of King James, Jonson produced nothing for the stage. But he "prosecuted" what he calls "his wonted studies" with such assiduity that he became in reality, as by report, one of the most learned men of his time. Jonson's theory of authorship involved a wide acquaintance with books and "an ability," as he put it, "to convert the substance or riches of another poet to his own use." Accordingly Jonson read not only the Greek and Latin classics down to the lesser writers, but he acquainted himself especially with the Latin writings of his learned contemporaries, their prose as well as their poetry, their antiquities and curious lore as well as their more solid learning. Though a poor man, Jonson was an indefatigable collector of books. He told Drummond that "the Earl of Pembroke sent him 20 pounds every first day of the new year to buy new books." Unhappily, in 1623, his library was destroyed by fire, an accident serio-comically described in his witty poem, "An Execration upon Vulcan." Yet even now a book turns up from time to time in which is inscribed, in fair large Italian lettering, the name, Ben Jonson. With respect to Jonson's use of his material, Dryden said memorably of him: "He was not only a professed imitator of Horace, but a learned plagiary of all the others; you track him everywhere in their snow....But he has done his robberies so openly that one sees he fears not to be taxed by any law. He invades authors like a monarch, and what would be theft in other poets is only victory in him." And yet it is but fair to say that Jonson prided himself, and justly, on his originality. In "Catiline," he not only uses

Sallust's account of the conspiracy, but he models some of the speeches of Cicero on the Roman orator's actual words. In "Poetaster," he lifts a whole satire out of Horace and dramatises it effectively for his purposes. The sophist Libanius suggests the situation of "The Silent Woman"; a Latin comedy of Giordano Bruno, "Il Candelaio," the relation of the dupes and the sharpers in "The Alchemist," the "Mostellaria" of Plautus, its admirable opening scene. But Jonson commonly bettered his sources, and putting the stamp of his sovereignty on whatever bullion he borrowed made it thenceforward to all time current and his own.

The lyric and especially the occasional poetry of Jonson has a peculiar merit. His theory demanded design and the perfection of literary finish. He was furthest from the rhapsodist and the careless singer of an idle day; and he believed that Apollo could only be worthily served in singing robes and laurel crowned. And yet many of Jonson's lyrics will live as long as the language. Who does not know "Queen and huntress, chaste and fair." "Drink to me only with thine eyes," or "Still to be neat, still to be dressed"? Beautiful in form, deft and graceful in expression, with not a word too much or one that bears not its part in the total effect, there is yet about the lyrics of Jonson a certain stiffness and formality, a suspicion that they were not quite spontaneous and unbidden, but that they were carved, so to speak, with disproportionate labour by a potent man of letters whose habitual thought is on greater things. It is for these reasons that Jonson is even better in the epigram and in occasional verse where rhetorical finish and pointed wit less interfere with the spontaneity and emotion which we usually associate with lyrical poetry. There are no such epitaphs as Ben Jonson's, witness the charming ones on his own children, on Salathiel Pavy, the child-actor, and many more; and this even though the rigid law of mine and thine must now restore to William Browne of Tavistock the famous lines beginning: "Underneath this sable hearse." Jonson is unsurpassed, too, in the difficult poetry of compliment, seldom falling into fulsome praise and disproportionate similitude, yet showing again and again a generous appreciation of worth in others, a discriminating taste and a generous personal regard. There was no man in England of his rank so well known and universally beloved as Ben Jonson. The list of his friends, of those to whom he had written verses, and those who had written verses to him, includes the name of every man of prominence in the England of King James. And the tone of many of these productions discloses an affectionate familiarity that speaks for the amiable personality and sound worth of the laureate. In 1619, growing unwieldy through inactivity, Jonson hit upon the heroic remedy of a journey afoot to Scotland. On his way thither and back he was hospitably received at the houses of many friends and by those to whom his friends had recommended him. When he arrived in Edinburgh, the burgesses met to grant him the freedom of the city, and Drummond, foremost of Scottish poets, was proud to entertain him for weeks as his guest at Hawthornden. Some of the noblest of Jonson's poems were inspired by friendship. Such is the fine "Ode to the memory of Sir Lucius Cary and Sir Henry Moryson," and that admirable piece of critical insight and filial affection, prefixed to the first Shakespeare folio, "To the memory of my beloved master, William Shakespeare, and what he hath left us," to mention only these. Nor can the earlier "Epode," beginning "Not to know vice at all," be matched in stately gravity and gnomic wisdom in its own wise and stately age.

But if Jonson had deserted the stage after the publication of his folio and up to the end of the reign of King James, he was far from inactive; for year after year his inexhaustible inventiveness continued to contribute to the masquing and entertainment at court. In "The Golden Age Restored," Pallas turns the Iron Age with its attendant evils into statues which sink out of sight; in "Pleasure Reconciled to Virtue," Atlas figures represented as an old man, his shoulders covered with snow, and Comus, "the god of cheer or the belly," is one of the characters, a circumstance which an imaginative boy of ten, named John Milton, was not to forget. "Pan's Anniversary," late in the reign of James, proclaimed that Jonson had not yet forgotten how to write exquisite lyrics, and "The Gipsies Metamorphosed" displayed the old drollery and broad humorous stroke still unimpaired and unmatchable. These, too, and the earlier years of Charles were the days of the Apollo Room of the

Devil Tavern where Jonson presided, the absolute monarch of English literary Bohemia. We hear of a room blazoned about with Jonson's own judicious "Leges Convivales" in letters of gold, of a company made up of the choicest spirits of the time, devotedly attached to their veteran dictator, his reminiscences, opinions, affections, and enmities. And we hear, too, of valorous potations; but in the words of Herrick addressed to his master, Jonson, at the Devil Tavern, as at the Dog, the Triple Tun, and at the Mermaid,

"We such clusters had
As made us nobly wild, not mad,
And yet each verse of thine
Outdid the meat, outdid the frolic wine."

But the patronage of the court failed in the days of King Charles, though Jonson was not without royal favours; and the old poet returned to the stage, producing, between 1625 and 1633, "The Staple of News," "The New Inn," "The Magnetic Lady," and "The Tale of a Tub," the last doubtless revised from a much earlier comedy. None of these plays met with any marked success, although the scathing generalisation of Dryden that designated them "Jonson's dotages" is unfair to their genuine merits. Thus the idea of an office for the gathering, proper dressing, and promulgation of news (wild flight of the fancy in its time) was an excellent subject for satire on the existing absurdities among newsmongers; although as much can hardly be said for "The Magnetic Lady," who, in her bounty, draws to her personages of differing humours to reconcile them in the end according to the alternative title, or "Humours Reconciled." These last plays of the old dramatist revert to caricature and the hard lines of allegory; the moralist is more than ever present, the satire degenerates into personal lampoon, especially of his sometime friend, Inigo Jones, who appears unworthily to have used his influence at court against the broken-down old poet. And now disease claimed Jonson, and he was bedridden for months. He had succeeded Middleton in 1628 as Chronologer to the City of London, but lost the post for not fulfilling its duties. King Charles befriended him, and even commissioned him to write still for the entertainment of the court; and he was not without the sustaining hand of noble patrons and devoted friends among the younger poets who were proud to be "sealed of the tribe of Ben."

Jonson died, August 6, 1637, and a second folio of his works, which he had been some time gathering, was printed in 1640, bearing in its various parts dates ranging from 1630 to 1642. It included all the plays mentioned in the foregoing paragraphs, excepting "The Case is Altered;" the masques, some fifteen, that date between 1617 and 1630; another collection of lyrics and occasional poetry called "Underwoods", including some further entertainments; a translation of "Horace's Art of Poetry" (also published in a vicesimo quarto in 1640), and certain fragments and ingatherings which the poet would hardly have included himself. These last comprise the fragment (less than seventy lines) of a tragedy called "Mortimer his Fall," and three acts of a pastoral drama of much beauty and poetic spirit, "The Sad Shepherd." There is also the exceedingly interesting "English Grammar" "made by Ben Jonson for the benefit of all strangers out of his observation of the English language now spoken and in use," in Latin and English; and "Timber, or Discoveries" "made upon men and matter as they have flowed out of his daily reading, or had their reflux to his peculiar notion of the times." The "Discoveries," as it is usually called, is a commonplace book such as many literary men have kept, in which their reading was chronicled, passages that took their fancy translated or transcribed, and their passing opinions noted. Many passages of Jonson's "Discoveries" are literal translations from the authors he chanced to be reading, with the reference, noted or not, as the accident of the moment prescribed. At times he follows the line of Macchiavelli's argument as to the nature and conduct of princes; at others he clarifies his own conception of poetry and poets by recourse to Aristotle. He finds a choice paragraph on eloquence in Seneca the elder and applies it to his own recollection of Bacon's power as an orator; and another on facile and ready genius, and translates it, adapting it to his recollection of his fellow-playwright, Shakespeare. To call such passages -- which Jonson never intended for publication -- plagiarism, is to obscure the significance of words. To disparage his memory by citing them is a preposterous use of scholarship. Jonson's prose, both in his dramas, in the descriptive comments of his masques, and in the "Discoveries," is characterised by clarity and vigorous directness, nor is it wanting in a fine sense of form or in the subtler graces of diction.

When Jonson died there was a project for a handsome monument to his memory. But the Civil War was at hand, and the project failed. A memorial, not insufficient, was carved on the stone covering his grave in one of the aisles of Westminster Abbey:

"O rare Ben Jonson."

Felix E. Schelling

A Glossary of Words & Meanings

In this modern day words and their meanings have evolved through many forms. Listed below are words commonly used by Jonson and his contemporaries and the meanings attributed to them then.

ABATE, cast down, subdue.

ABHORRING, repugnant (to), at variance.

ABJECT, base, degraded thing, outcast.

ABRASE, smooth, blank.

ABSOLUTE(LY), faultless(ly).

ABSTRACTED, abstract, abstruse.

ABUSE, deceive, insult, dishonour, make ill use of.

ACATER, caterer.

ACATES, cates.

ACCEPTIVE, willing, ready to accept, receive.

ACCOMMODATE, fit, befitting. (The word was a fashionable one and used on all occasions. See "Henry IV.," pt. 2, iii. 4).

ACCOST, draw near, approach.

ACKNOWN, confessedly acquainted with.

ACME, full maturity.

ADALANTADO, lord deputy or governor of a Spanish province.

ADJECTION, addition.

ADMIRATION, astonishment.

ADMIRE, wonder, wonder at.

ADROP, philosopher's stone, or substance from which obtained.

ADSCRIVE, subscribe.

ADULTERATE, spurious, counterfeit.

ADVANCE, lift.

ADVERTISE, inform, give intelligence.

ADVERTISED, "be—," be it known to you.

ADVERTISEMENT, intelligence.

ADVISE, consider, bethink oneself, deliberate.

ADVISED, informed, aware; "are you—?" have you found that out?

AFFECT, love, like; aim at; move.

AFFECTED, disposed; beloved.

AFFECTIONATE, obstinate; prejudiced.

AFFECTS, affections.

AFFRONT, "give the—," face.

AFFY, have confidence in; betroth.

AFTER, after the manner of.

AGAIN, AGAINST, in anticipation of.

AGGRAVATE, increase, magnify, enlarge upon.

AGNOMINATION. See Paranomasie.

AIERY, nest, brood.

AIM, guess.

ALL HID, children's cry at hide-and-seek.

ALL-TO, completely, entirely ("all-to-be-laden").

ALLOWANCE, approbation, recognition.

ALMA-CANTARAS (astronomy), parallels of altitude.

ALMAIN, name of a dance.

ALMUTEN, planet of chief influence in the horoscope.

ALONE, unequalled, without peer.

ALUDELS, subliming pots.

AMAZED, confused, perplexed.

AMBER, AMBRE, ambergris.

AMBREE, MARY, a woman noted for her valour at the siege of Ghent, 1458.

AMES-ACE, lowest throw at dice.

AMPHIBOLIES, ambiguities.

AMUSED, bewildered, amazed.

AN, if.

ANATOMY, skeleton, or dissected body.

ANDIRONS, fire-dogs.

ANGEL, gold coin worth 10 shillings, stamped with the figure of the archangel Michael.

ANNESH CLEARE, spring known as Agnes le Clare.

ANSWER, return hit in fencing.

ANTIC, ANTIQUE, clown, buffoon.

ANTIC, like a buffoon.

ANTIPERISTASIS, an opposition which enhances the quality it opposes.

APOZEM, decoction.

APPERIL, peril.

APPLE-JOHN, APPLE-SQUIRE, pimp, pander.

APPLY, attach.

APPREHEND, take into custody.

APPREHENSIVE, quick of perception; able to perceive and appreciate.

APPROVE, prove, confirm.

APT, suit, adapt; train, prepare; dispose, incline.

APT(LY), suitable(y), opportune(ly).

APTITUDE, suitableness.

ARBOR, "make the—," cut up the game (Gifford).

ARCHES, Court of Arches.

ARCHIE, Archibald Armstrong, jester to James I. and Charles I.

ARGAILE, argol, crust or sediment in wine casks.

ARGENT-VIVE, quicksilver.

ARGUMENT, plot of a drama; theme, subject; matter in question; token, proof.

ARRIDE, please.

ARSEDINE, mixture of copper and zinc, used as an imitation of gold-leaf.

ARTHUR, PRINCE, reference to an archery show by a society who assumed arms, etc., of Arthur's knights.

ARTICLE, item.

ARTIFICIALLY, artfully.

ASCENSION, evaporation, distillation.

ASPIRE, try to reach, obtain, long for.

ASSALTO (Italian), assault.

ASSAY, draw a knife along the belly of the deer, a ceremony of the hunting-field.

ASSOIL, solve.

ASSURE, secure possession or reversion of.

ATHANOR, a digesting furnace, calculated to keep up a constant heat.

ATONE, reconcile.

ATTACH, attack, seize.

AUDACIOUS, having spirit and confidence.

AUTHENTIC(AL), of authority, authorised, trustworthy, genuine.

AVISEMENT, reflection, consideration.

AVOID, begone! get rid of.

AWAY WITH, endure.

AZOCH, Mercurius Philosophorum.

BABION, baboon.

BABY, doll.

BACK-SIDE, back premises.

BAFFLE, treat with contempt.

BAGATINE, Italian coin, worth about the third of a farthing.

BAIARD, horse of magic powers known to old romance.

BALDRICK, belt worn across the breast to support bugle, etc.

BALE (of dice), pair.

BALK, overlook, pass by, avoid.

BALLACE, ballast.

BALLOO, game at ball.

BALNEUM (BAIN MARIE), a vessel for holding hot water in which other vessels are stood for heating.

BANBURY, "brother of—," Puritan.

BANDOG, dog tied or chained up.

BANE, woe, ruin.

BANQUET, a light repast; dessert.

BARB, to clip gold.

BARBEL, fresh-water fish.

BARE, meer; bareheaded; it was "a particular mark of state and grandeur for the coachman to be uncovered" (Gifford).

BARLEY-BREAK, game somewhat similar to base.

BASE, game of prisoner's base.

BASES, richly embroidered skirt reaching to the knees, or lower.

BASILISK, fabulous reptile, believed to slay with its eye.

BASKET, used for the broken provision collected for prisoners.

BASON, basons, etc., were beaten by the attendant mob when bad characters were "carted."

BATE, be reduced; abate, reduce.

BATOON, baton, stick.

BATTEN, feed, grow fat.

BAWSON, badger.

BEADSMAN, prayer-man, one engaged to pray for another.

BEAGLE, small hound; fig. spy.

BEAR IN HAND, keep in suspense, deceive with false hopes.

BEARWARD, bear leader.

BEDPHERE. See Phere.

BEDSTAFF, (?) wooden pin in the side of the bedstead for supporting the bedclothes (Johnson); one of the sticks or "laths"; a stick used in making a bed.

BEETLE, heavy mallet.

BEG, "I'd—him," the custody of minors and idiots was begged for; likewise property fallen forfeit to the Crown ("your house had been begged").

BELL-MAN, night watchman.

BENJAMIN, an aromatic gum.

BERLINA, pillory.

BESCUMBER, defile.

BESLAVE, beslabber.

BESOGNO, beggar.

BESPAWLE, bespatter.

BETHLEHEM GABOR, Transylvanian hero, proclaimed King of Hungary.

BEVER, drinking.

BEVIS, SIR, knight of romance whose horse was equally celebrated.

BEWRAY, reveal, make known.

BEZANT, heraldic term: small gold circle.

BEZOAR'S STONE, a remedy known by this name was a supposed antidote to poison.

BID-STAND, highwayman.

BIGGIN, cap, similar to that worn by the Beguines; nightcap.

BILIVE (belive), with haste.

BILK, nothing, empty talk.

BILL, kind of pike.

BILLET, wood cut for fuel, stick.

BIRDING, thieving.

BLACK SANCTUS, burlesque hymn, any unholy riot.

BLANK, originally a small French coin.

BLANK, white.

BLANKET, toss in a blanket.

BLAZE, outburst of violence.

BLAZE, (her.) blazon; publish abroad.

BLAZON, armorial bearings; fig. all that pertains to good birth and breeding.

BLIN, "withouten—," without ceasing.

BLOW, puff up.

BLUE, colour of servants' livery, hence "—order," "—waiters."

BLUSHET, blushing one.

BOB, jest, taunt.

BOB, beat, thump.

BODGE, measure.

BODKIN, dagger, or other short, pointed weapon; long pin with which the women fastened up their hair.

BOLT, roll (of material).

BOLT, dislodge, rout out; sift (boulting-tub).

BOLT'S-HEAD, long, straight-necked vessel for distillation.

BOMBARD SLOPS, padded, puffed-out breeches.

BONA ROBA, "good, wholesome, plum-cheeked wench" (Johnson) —not always used in compliment.

BONNY-CLABBER, sour butter-milk.

BOOKHOLDER, prompter.

BOOT, "to—," into the bargain; "no—," of no avail.

BORACHIO, bottle made of skin.

BORDELLO, brothel.

BORNE IT, conducted, carried it through.

BOTTLE (of hay), bundle, truss.

BOTTOM, skein or ball of thread; vessel.

BOURD, jest.

BOVOLI, snails or cockles dressed in the Italian manner (Gifford).

BOW-POT, flower vase or pot.

BOYS, "terrible—," "angry—," roystering young bucks. (See Nares).

BRABBLES (BRABBLESH), brawls.

BRACH, bitch.

BRADAMANTE, a heroine in "Orlando Furioso."

BRADLEY, ARTHUR OF, a lively character commemorated in ballads.

BRAKE, frame for confining a horse's feet while being shod, or strong curb or bridle; trap.

BRANCHED, with "detached sleeve ornaments, projecting from the shoulders of the gown" (Gifford).

BRANDISH, flourish of weapon.

BRASH, brace.

BRAVE, bravado, braggart speech.

BRAVE (adv.), gaily, finely (apparelled).

BRAVERIES, gallants.

BRAVERY, extravagant gaiety of apparel.

BRAVO, bravado, swaggerer.

BRAZEN-HEAD, speaking head made by Roger Bacon.

BREATHE, pause for relaxation; exercise.

BREATH UPON, speak dispraisingly of.

BREND, burn.

BRIDE-ALE, wedding feast.

BRIEF, abstract; (mus.) breve.

BRISK, smartly dressed.

BRIZE, breese, gadfly.

BROAD-SEAL, state seal.

BROCK, badger (term of contempt).

BROKE, transact business as a broker.

BROOK, endure, put up with.

BROUGHTON, HUGH, an English divine and Hebrew scholar.

BRUIT, rumour.

BUCK, wash.

BUCKLE, bend.

BUFF, leather made of buffalo skin, used for military and serjeants' coats, etc.

BUFO, black tincture.

BUGLE, long-shaped bead.

BULLED, (?) bolled, swelled.

BULLIONS, trunk hose.

BULLY, term of familiar endearment.

BUNGY, Friar Bungay, who had a familiar in the shape of a dog.

BURDEN, refrain, chorus.

BURGONET, closely-fitting helmet with visor.

BURGULLION, braggadocio.

BURN, mark wooden measures ("—ing of cans").

BURROUGH, pledge, security.

BUSKIN, half-boot, foot gear reaching high up the leg.

BUTT-SHAFT, barbless arrow for shooting at butts.

BUTTER, NATHANIEL ("Staple of News"), a compiler of general news. (See Cunningham).

BUTTERY-HATCH, half-door shutting off the buttery, where provisions and liquors were stored.

BUY, "he bought me," formerly the guardianship of wards could be bought.

BUZ, exclamation to enjoin silence.

BUZZARD, simpleton.

BY AND BY, at once.

BY(E), "on the __," incidentally, as of minor or secondary importance; at the side.

BY-CHOP, by-blow, bastard.

CADUCEUS, Mercury's wand.

CALIVER, light kind of musket.

CALLET, woman of ill repute.

CALLOT, coif worn on the wigs of our judges or serjeants-at-law (Gifford).

CALVERED, crimped, or sliced and pickled. (See Nares).

CAMOUCCIO, wretch, knave.

CAMUSED, flat.

CAN, knows.

CANDLE-RENT, rent from house property.

CANDLE-WASTER, one who studies late.

CANTER, sturdy beggar.

CAP OF MAINTENCE, an insignia of dignity, a cap of state borne before kings at their coronation; also an heraldic term.

CAPABLE, able to comprehend, fit to receive instruction, impression.

CAPANEUS, one of the "Seven against Thebes."

CARACT, carat, unit of weight for precious stones, etc.; value, worth.

CARANZA, Spanish author of a book on duelling.

CARCANET, jewelled ornament for the neck.

CARE, take care; object.

CAROSH, coach, carriage.

CARPET, table-cover.

CARRIAGE, bearing, behaviour.

CARWHITCHET, quip, pun.

CASAMATE, casemate, fortress.

CASE, a pair.

CASE, "in—," in condition.

CASSOCK, soldier's loose overcoat.

CAST, flight of hawks, couple.

CAST, throw dice; vomit; forecast, calculate.

CAST, cashiered.

CASTING-GLASS, bottle for sprinkling perfume.

CASTRIL, kestrel, falcon.

CAT, structure used in sieges.

CATAMITE, old form of "ganymede."

CATASTROPHE, conclusion.

CATCHPOLE, sheriff's officer.

CATES, dainties, provisions.

CATSO, rogue, cheat.

CAUTELOUS, crafty, artful.

CENSURE, criticism; sentence.

CENSURE, criticise; pass sentence, doom.

CERUSE, cosmetic containing white lead.

CESS, assess.

CHANGE, "hunt—," follow a fresh scent.

CHAPMAN, retail dealer.

CHARACTER, handwriting.

CHARGE, expense.

CHARM, subdue with magic, lay a spell on, silence.

CHARMING, exercising magic power.

CHARTEL, challenge.

CHEAP, bargain, market.

CHEAR, CHEER, comfort, encouragement; food, entertainment.

CHECK AT, aim reproof at.

CHEQUIN, gold Italian coin.

CHEVRIL, from kidskin, which is elastic and pliable.

CHIAUS, Turkish envoy; used for a cheat, swindler.

CHILDERMASS DAY, Innocents' Day.

CHOKE-BAIL, action which does not allow of bail.

CHRYSOPOEIA, alchemy.

CHRYSOSPERM, ways of producing gold.

CIBATION, adding fresh substances to supply the waste of evaporation.

CIMICI, bugs.

CINOPER, cinnabar.

CIOPPINI, chopine, lady's high shoe.

CIRCLING BOY, "a species of roarer; one who in some way drew a man into a snare, to cheat or rob him" (Nares).

CIRCUMSTANCE, circumlocution, beating about the bush; ceremony, everything pertaining to a certain condition; detail, particular.

CITRONISE, turn citron colour.

CITTERN, kind of guitar.

CITY-WIRES, woman of fashion, who made use of wires for hair and dress.

CIVIL, legal.

CLAP, clack, chatter.

CLAPPER-DUDGEON, downright beggar.

CLAPS HIS DISH, a clap, or clack, dish (dish with a movable lid) was carried by beggars and lepers to show that the vessel was empty, and to give sound of their approach.

CLARIDIANA, heroine of an old romance.

CLARISSIMO, Venetian noble.

CLEM, starve.

CLICKET, latch.

CLIM O' THE CLOUGHS, etc., wordy heroes of romance.

CLIMATE, country.

CLOSE, secret, private; secretive.

CLOSENESS, secrecy.

CLOTH, arras, hangings.

CLOUT, mark shot at, bull's eye.

CLOWN, countryman, clodhopper.

COACH-LEAVES, folding blinds.

COALS, "bear no—," submit to no affront.

COAT-ARMOUR, coat of arms.

COAT-CARD, court-card.

COB-HERRING, HERRING-COB, a young herring.

COB-SWAN, male swan.

COCK-A-HOOP, denoting unstinted jollity; thought to be derived from turning on the tap that all might drink to the full of the flowing liquor.

COCKATRICE, reptile supposed to be produced from a cock's egg and to kill by its eye—used as a term of reproach for a woman.

COCK-BRAINED, giddy, wild.

COCKER, pamper.

COCKSCOMB, fool's cap.

COCKSTONE, stone said to be found in a cock's gizzard, and to possess particular virtues.

CODLING, softening by boiling.

COFFIN, raised crust of a pie.

COG, cheat, wheedle.

COIL, turmoil, confusion, ado.

COKELY, master of a puppet-show (Whalley).

COKES, fool, gull.

COLD-CONCEITED, having cold opinion of, coldly affected towards.

COLE-HARBOUR, a retreat for people of all sorts.

COLLECTION, composure; deduction.

COLLOP, small slice, piece of flesh.

COLLY, blacken.

COLOUR, pretext.

COLOURS, "fear no—," no enemy (quibble).

COLSTAFF, cowlstaff, pole for carrying a cowl=tub.

COME ABOUT, charge, turn round.

COMFORTABLE BREAD, spiced gingerbread.

COMING, forward, ready to respond, complaisant.

COMMENT, commentary; "sometime it is taken for a lie or fayned tale" (Bullokar, 1616).

COMMODITY, "current for—," allusion to practice of money-lenders, who forced the borrower to take part of the loan in the shape of worthless goods on which the latter had to make money if he could.

COMMUNICATE, share.

COMPASS, "in—," within the range, sphere.

COMPLEMENT, completion, completement; anything required for the perfecting or carrying out of a person or affair; accomplishment.

COMPLEXION, natural disposition, constitution.

COMPLIMENT, See Complement.

COMPLIMENTARIES, masters of accomplishments.

COMPOSITION, constitution; agreement, contract.

COMPOSURE, composition.

COMPTER, COUNTER, debtors' prison.

CONCEALMENT, a certain amount of church property had been retained at the dissolution of the monasteries; Elizabeth sent commissioners to search it out, and the courtiers begged for it.

CONCEIT, idea, fancy, witty invention, conception, opinion.

CONCEIT, apprehend.

CONCEITED, fancifully, ingeniously devised or conceived; possessed of intelligence, witty, ingenious (hence well conceited, etc.); disposed to joke; of opinion, possessed of an idea.

CONCEIVE, understand.

CONCENT, harmony, agreement.

CONCLUDE, infer, prove.

CONCOCT, assimilate, digest.

CONDEN'T, probably conducted.

CONDUCT, escort, conductor.

CONEY-CATCH, cheat.

CONFECT, sweetmeat.

CONFER, compare.

CONGIES, bows.

CONNIVE, give a look, wink, of secret intelligence.

CONSORT, company, concert.

CONSTANCY, fidelity, ardour, persistence.

CONSTANT, confIrmed, persistent, faithful.

CONSTANTLY, firmly, persistently.

CONTEND, strive.

CONTINENT, holding together.

CONTROL (the point), bear or beat down.

CONVENT, assembly, meeting.

CONVERT, turn (oneself).

CONVEY, transmit from one to another.

CONVINCE, evince, prove; overcome, overpower; convict.

COP, head, top; tuft on head of birds; "a cop" may have reference to one or other meaning; Gifford and others interpret as "conical, terminating in a point."

COPE-MAN, chapman.

COPESMATE, companion.

COPY (Lat. copia), abundance, copiousness.

CORN ("powder—"), grain.

COROLLARY, finishing part or touch.

CORSIVE, corrosive.

CORTINE, curtain, (arch.) wall between two towers, etc.

CORYAT, famous for his travels, published as "Coryat's Crudities."

COSSET, pet lamb, pet.

COSTARD, head.

COSTARD-MONGER, apple-seller, coster-monger.

COSTS, ribs.

COTE, hut.

COTHURNAL, from "cothurnus," a particular boot worn by actors in Greek tragedy.

COTQUEAN, hussy.

COUNSEL, secret.

COUNTENANCE, means necessary for support; credit, standing.

COUNTER. See Compter.

COUNTER, pieces of metal or ivory for calculating at play.

COUNTER, "hunt—," follow scent in reverse direction.

COUNTERFEIT, false coin.

COUNTERPANE, one part or counterpart of a deed or indenture.

COUNTERPOINT, opposite, contrary point.

COURT-DISH, a kind of drinking-cup (Halliwell); N.E.D. quotes from Bp. Goodman's "Court of James I.": "The king... caused his carver to cut him out a court-dish, that is, something of every dish, which he sent him as part of his reversion," but this does not sound like short allowance or small receptacle.

COURT-DOR, fool.

COURTEAU, curtal, small horse with docked tail.

COURTSHIP, courtliness.

COVETISE, avarice.

COWSHARD, cow dung.

COXCOMB, fool's cap, fool.

COY, shrink; disdain.

COYSTREL, low varlet.

COZEN, cheat.

CRACK, lively young rogue, wag.

CRACK, crack up, boast; come to grief.

CRAMBE, game of crambo, in which the players find rhymes for a given word.

CRANCH, craunch.

CRANION, spider-like; also fairy appellation for a fly (Gifford, who refers to lines in Drayton's "Nimphidia").

CRIMP, game at cards.

CRINCLE, draw back, turn aside.

CRISPED, with curled or waved hair.

CROP, gather, reap.

CROPSHIRE, a kind of herring. (See N.E.D.)

CROSS, any piece of money, many coins being stamped with a cross.

CROSS AND PILE, heads and tails.

CROSSLET, crucible.

CROWD, fiddle.

CRUDITIES, undigested matter.

CRUMP, curl up.

CRUSADO, Portuguese gold coin, marked with a cross.

CRY ("he that cried Italian"), "speak in a musical cadence," intone, or declaim (?); cry up.

CUCKING-STOOL, used for the ducking of scolds, etc.

CUCURBITE, a gourd-shaped vessel used for distillation.

CUERPO, "in—," in undress.

CULLICE, broth.

CULLION, base fellow, coward.

CULLISEN, badge worn on their arm by servants.

CULVERIN, kind of cannon.

CUNNING, skill.

CUNNING, skilful.

CUNNING-MAN, fortune-teller.

CURE, care for.

CURIOUS(LY), scrupulous, particular; elaborate, elegant(ly), dainty(ly) (hence "in curious").

CURST, shrewish, mischievous.

CURTAL, dog with docked tail, of inferior sort.

CUSTARD, "quaking—," "—politic," reference to a large custard which formed part of a city feast and afforded huge entertainment, for the fool jumped into it, and other like tricks were played. (See "All's Well, etc." ii. 5, 40.)

CUTWORK, embroidery, open-work.

CYPRES (CYPRUS) (quibble), cypress (or cyprus) being a transparent material, and when black used for mourning.

DAGGER ("—frumety"), name of tavern.

DARGISON, apparently some person known in ballad or tale.

DAUPHIN MY BOY, refrain of old comic song.

DAW, daunt.

DEAD LIFT, desperate emergency.

DEAR, applied to that which in any way touches us nearly.

DECLINE, turn off from; turn away, aside.

DEFALK, deduct, abate.

DEFEND, forbid.

DEGENEROUS, degenerate.

DEGREES, steps.

DELATE, accuse.

DEMI-CULVERIN, cannon carrying a ball of about ten pounds.

DENIER, the smallest possible coin, being the twelfth part of a sou.

DEPART, part with.

DEPENDANCE, ground of quarrel in duello language.

DESERT, reward.

DESIGNMENT, design.

DESPERATE, rash, reckless.

DETECT, allow to be detected, betray, inform against.

DETERMINE, terminate.

DETRACT, draw back, refuse.

DEVICE, masque, show; a thing moved by wires, etc., puppet.

DEVISE, exact in every particular.

DEVISED, invented.

DIAPASM, powdered aromatic herbs, made into balls of perfumed paste. (See Pomander.)

DIBBLE, (?) moustache (N.E.D.); (?) dagger (Cunningham).

DIFFUSED, disordered, scattered, irregular.

DIGHT, dressed.

DILDO, refrain of popular songs; vague term of low meaning.

DIMBLE, dingle, ravine.

DIMENSUM, stated allowance.

DISBASE, debase.

DISCERN, distinguish, show a difference between.

DISCHARGE, settle for.

DISCIPLINE, reformation; ecclesiastical system.

DISCLAIM, renounce all part in.

DISCOURSE, process of reasoning, reasoning faculty.

DISCOURTSHIP, discourtesy.

DISCOVER, betray, reveal; display.

DISFAVOUR, disfigure.

DISPARAGEMENT, legal term applied to the unfitness in any way of a marriage arranged for in the case of wards.

DISPENSE WITH, grant dispensation for.

DISPLAY, extend.

DIS'PLE, discipline, teach by the whip.

DISPOSED, inclined to merriment.

DISPOSURE, disposal.

DISPRISE, depreciate.

DISPUNCT, not punctilious.

DISQUISITION, search.

DISSOLVED, enervated by grief.

DISTANCE, (?) proper measure.

DISTASTE, offence, cause of offence.

DISTASTE, render distasteful.

DISTEMPERED, upset, out of humour.

DIVISION (mus.), variation, modulation.

DOG-BOLT, term of contempt.

DOLE, given in dole, charity.

DOLE OF FACES, distribution of grimaces.

DOOM, verdict, sentence.

DOP, dip, low bow.

DOR, beetle, buzzing insect, drone, idler.

DOR, (?) buzz; "give the—," make a fool of.

DOSSER, pannier, basket.

DOTES, endowments, qualities.

DOTTEREL, plover; gull, fool.

DOUBLE, behave deceitfully.

DOXY, wench, mistress.

DRACHM, Greek silver coin.

DRESS, groom, curry.

DRESSING, coiffure.

DRIFT, intention.

DRYFOOT, track by mere scent of foot.

DUCKING, punishment for minor offences.

DUILL, grieve.

DUMPS, melancholy, originally a mournful melody.

DURINDANA, Orlando's sword.

DWINDLE, shrink away, be overawed.

EAN, yean, bring forth young.

EASINESS, readiness.

EBOLITION, ebullition.

EDGE, sword.

EECH, eke.

EGREGIOUS, eminently excellent.

EKE, also, moreover.

E-LA, highest note in the scale.

EGGS ON THE SPIT, important business on hand.

ELF-LOCK, tangled hair, supposed to be the work of elves.

EMMET, ant.

ENGAGE, involve.

ENGHLE. See Ingle.

ENGHLE, cajole; fondle.

ENGIN(E), device, contrivance; agent; ingenuity, wit.

ENGINER, engineer, deviser, plotter.

ENGINOUS, crafty, full of devices; witty, ingenious.

ENGROSS, monopolise.

ENS, an existing thing, a substance.

ENSIGNS, tokens, wounds.

ENSURE, assure.

ENTERTAIN, take into service.

ENTREAT, plead.

ENTREATY, entertainment.

ENTRY, place where a deer has lately passed.

ENVOY, denouement, conclusion.

ENVY, spite, calumny, dislike, odium.

EPHEMERIDES, calendars.

EQUAL, just, impartial.

ERECTION, elevation in esteem.

ERINGO, candied root of the sea-holly, formerly used as a sweetmeat and aphrodisiac.

ERRANT, arrant.

ESSENTIATE, become assimilated.

ESTIMATION, esteem.

ESTRICH, ostrich.

ETHNIC, heathen.

EURIPUS, flux and reflux.

EVEN, just equable.

EVENT, fate, issue.

EVENT(ED), issue(d).

EVERT, overturn.

EXACUATE, sharpen.

EXAMPLESS, without example or parallel.

EXCALIBUR, King Arthur's sword.

EXEMPLIFY, make an example of.

EXEMPT, separate, exclude.

EXEQUIES, obsequies.

EXHALE, drag out.

EXHIBITION, allowance for keep, pocket-money.

EXORBITANT, exceeding limits of propriety or law, inordinate.

EXORNATION, ornament.

EXPECT, wait.

EXPIATE, terminate.

EXPLICATE, explain, unfold.

EXTEMPORAL, extempore, unpremeditated.

EXTRACTION, essence.

EXTRAORDINARY, employed for a special or temporary purpose.

EXTRUDE, expel.

EYE, "in—," in view.

EYEBRIGHT, (?) a malt liquor in which the herb of this name was infused, or a person who sold the same (Gifford).

EYE-TINGE, least shade or gleam.

FACE, appearance.

FACES ABOUT, military word of command.

FACINOROUS, extremely wicked.

FACKINGS, faith.

FACT, deed, act, crime.

FACTIOUS, seditious, belonging to a party, given to party feeling.

FAECES, dregs.

FAGIOLI, French beans.

FAIN, forced, necessitated.

FAITHFUL, believing.

FALL, ruff or band turned back on the shoulders; or, veil.

FALSIFY, feign (fencing term).

FAME, report.

FAMILIAR, attendant spirit.

FANTASTICAL, capricious, whimsical.

FARCE, stuff.

FAR-FET. See Fet.

FARTHINGAL, hooped petticoat.

FAUCET, tapster.

FAULT, lack; loss, break in line of scent; "for—," in default of.

FAUTOR, partisan.

FAYLES, old table game similar to backgammon.

FEAR(ED), affright(ed).

FEAT, activity, operation; deed, action.

FEAT, elegant, trim.

FEE, "in—" by feudal obligation.

FEIZE, beat, belabour.

FELLOW, term of contempt.

FENNEL, emblem of flattery.

FERE, companion, fellow.

FERN-SEED, supposed to have power of rendering invisible.

FET, fetched.

FETCH, trick.

FEUTERER (Fr. vautrier), dog-keeper.

FEWMETS, dung.

FICO, fig.

FIGGUM, (?) jugglery.

FIGMENT, fiction, invention.

FIRK, frisk, move suddenly, or in jerks; "—up," stir up, rouse; "firks mad," suddenly behaves like a madman.

FIT, pay one out, punish.

FITNESS, readiness.

FITTON (FITTEN), lie, invention.

FIVE-AND-FIFTY, "highest number to stand on at primero" (Gifford).

FLAG, to fly low and waveringly.

FLAGON CHAIN, for hanging a smelling-bottle (Fr. flacon) round the neck (?). (See N.E.D.).

FLAP-DRAGON, game similar to snap-dragon.

FLASKET, some kind of basket.

FLAW, sudden gust or squall of wind.

FLAWN, custard.

FLEA, catch fleas.

FLEER, sneer, laugh derisively.

FLESH, feed a hawk or dog with flesh to incite it to the chase; initiate in blood-shed; satiate.

FLICKER-MOUSE, bat.

FLIGHT, light arrow.

FLITTER-MOUSE, bat.

FLOUT, mock, speak and act contemptuously.

FLOWERS, pulverised substance.

FLY, familiar spirit.

FOIL, weapon used in fencing; that which sets anything off to advantage.

FOIST, cut-purse, sharper.

FOND(LY), foolish(ly).

FOOT-CLOTH, housings of ornamental cloth which hung down on either side a horse to the ground.

FOOTING, foothold; footstep; dancing.

FOPPERY, foolery.

FOR, "—failing," for fear of failing.

FORBEAR, bear with; abstain from.

FORCE, "hunt at—," run the game down with dogs.

FOREHEAD, modesty; face, assurance, effrontery.

FORESLOW, delay.

FORESPEAK, bewitch; foretell.

FORETOP, front lock of hair which fashion required to be worn upright.

FORGED, fabricated.

FORM, state formally.

FORMAL, shapely; normal; conventional.

FORTHCOMING, produced when required.

FOUNDER, disable with over-riding.

FOURM, form, lair.

FOX, sword.

FRAIL, rush basket in which figs or raisins were packed.

FRAMPULL, peevish, sour-tempered.

FRAPLER, blusterer, wrangler.

FRAYING, "a stag is said to fray his head when he rubs it against a tree to... cause the outward coat of the new horns to fall off" (Gifford).

FREIGHT (of the gazetti), burden (of the newspapers).

FREQUENT, full.

FRICACE, rubbing.

FRICATRICE, woman of low character.

FRIPPERY, old clothes shop.

FROCK, smock-frock.

FROLICS, (?) humorous verses circulated at a feast (N.E.D.); couplets wrapped round sweetmeats (Cunningham).

FRONTLESS, shameless.

FROTED, rubbed.

FRUMETY, hulled wheat boiled in milk and spiced.

FRUMP, flout, sneer.

FUCUS, dye.

FUGEAND, (?) figent: fidgety, restless (N.E.D.).

FULLAM, false dice.

FULMART, polecat.

FULSOME, foul, offensive.

FURIBUND, raging, furious.

GALLEY-FOIST, city-barge, used on Lord Mayor's Day, when he was sworn into his office at Westminster (Whalley).

GALLIARD, lively dance in triple time.

GAPE, be eager after.

GARAGANTUA, Rabelais' giant.

GARB, sheaf (Fr. gerbe); manner, fashion, behaviour.

GARD, guard, trimming, gold or silver lace, or other ornament.

GARDED, faced or trimmed.

GARNISH, fee.

GAVEL-KIND, name of a land-tenure existing chiefly in Kent; from 16th century often used to denote custom of dividing a deceased man's property equally among his sons (N.E.D.).

GAZETTE, small Venetian coin worth about three-farthings.

GEANCE, jaunt, errand.

GEAR (GEER), stuff, matter, affair.

GELID, frozen.

GEMONIES, steps from which the bodies of criminals were thrown into the river.

GENERAL, free, affable.

GENIUS, attendant spirit.

GENTRY, gentlemen; manners characteristic of gentry, good breeding.

GIB-CAT, tom-cat.

GIGANTOMACHIZE, start a giants' war.

GIGLOT, wanton.

GIMBLET, gimlet.

GING, gang.

GLASS ("taking in of shadows, etc."), crystal or beryl.

GLEEK, card game played by three; party of three, trio; side glance.

GLICK (GLEEK), jest, gibe.

GLIDDER, glaze.

GLORIOUSLY, of vain glory.

GODWIT, bird of the snipe family.

GOLD-END-MAN, a buyer of broken gold and silver.

GOLL, hand.

GONFALIONIER, standard-bearer, chief magistrate, etc.

GOOD, sound in credit.

GOOD-YEAR, good luck.

GOOSE-TURD, colour of. (See Turd).

GORCROW, carrion crow.

GORGET, neck armour.

GOSSIP, godfather.

GOWKED, from "gowk," to stand staring and gaping like a fool.

GRANNAM, grandam.

GRASS, (?) grease, fat.

GRATEFUL, agreeable, welcome.

GRATIFY, give thanks to.

GRATITUDE, gratuity.

GRATULATE, welcome, congratulate.

GRAVITY, dignity.

GRAY, badger.

GRICE, cub.

GRIEF, grievance.

GRIPE, vulture, griffin.

GRIPE'S EGG, vessel in shape of.

GROAT, fourpence.

GROGRAN, coarse stuff made of silk and mohair, or of coarse silk.

GROOM-PORTER, officer in the royal household.

GROPE, handle, probe.

GROUND, pit (hence "grounded judgments").

GUARD, caution, heed.

GUARDANT, heraldic term: turning the head only.

GUILDER, Dutch coin worth about 4d.

GULES, gullet, throat; heraldic term for red.

GULL, simpleton, dupe.

GUST, taste.

HAB NAB, by, on, chance.

HABERGEON, coat of mail.

HAGGARD, wild female hawk; hence coy, wild.

HALBERD, combination of lance and battle-axe.

HALL, "a—!" a cry to clear the room for the dancers.

HANDSEL, first money taken.

HANGER, loop or strap on a sword-belt from which the sword was suspended.

HAP, fortune, luck.

HAPPILY, haply.

HAPPINESS, appropriateness, fitness.

HAPPY, rich.

HARBOUR, track, trace (an animal) to its shelter.

HARD-FAVOURED, harsh-featured.

HARPOCRATES, Horus the child, son of Osiris, figured with a finger pointing to his mouth, indicative of silence.

HARRINGTON, a patent was granted to Lord H. for the coinage of tokens (q.v.).

HARROT, herald.

HARRY NICHOLAS, founder of a community called the "Family of Love."

HAY, net for catching rabbits, etc.

HAY! (Ital. hai!), you have it (a fencing term).

HAY IN HIS HORN, ill-tempered person.

HAZARD, game at dice; that which is staked.

HEAD, "first—," young deer with antlers first sprouting; fig. a newly-ennobled man.

HEADBOROUGH, constable.

HEARKEN AFTER, inquire; "hearken out," find, search out.

HEARTEN, encourage.

HEAVEN AND HELL ("Alchemist"), names of taverns.

HECTIC, fever.

HEDGE IN, include.

HELM, upper part of a retort.

HER'NSEW, hernshaw, heron.

HIERONIMO (JERONIMO), hero of Kyd's "Spanish Tragedy."

HOBBY, nag.

HOBBY-HORSE, imitation horse of some light material, fastened round the waist of the morrice-dancer, who imitated the movements of a skittish horse.

HODDY-DODDY, fool.

HOIDEN, hoyden, formerly applied to both sexes (ancient term for leveret? Gifford).

HOLLAND, name of two famous chemists.

HONE AND HONERO, wailing expressions of lament or discontent.

HOOD-WINK'D, blindfolded.

HORARY, hourly.

HORN-MAD, stark mad (quibble).

HORN-THUMB, cut-purses were in the habit of wearing a horn shield on the thumb.

HORSE-BREAD-EATING, horses were often fed on coarse bread.

HORSE-COURSER, horse-dealer.

HOSPITAL, Christ's Hospital.

HOWLEGLAS, Eulenspiegel, the hero of a popular German tale which relates his buffooneries and knavish tricks.

HUFF, hectoring, arrogance.

HUFF IT, swagger.

HUISHER (Fr. huissier), usher.

HUM, beer and spirits mixed together.

HUMANITIAN, humanist, scholar.

HUMOROUS, capricious, moody, out of humour; moist.

HUMOUR, a word used in and out of season in the time of Shakespeare and Ben Jonson, and ridiculed by both.

HUMOURS, manners.

HUMPHREY, DUKE, those who were dinnerless spent the dinner-hour in a part of St. Paul's where stood a monument said to be that of the duke's; hence "dine with Duke Humphrey," to go hungry.

HURTLESS, harmless.

IDLE, useless, unprofitable.

ILL-AFFECTED, ill-disposed.

ILL-HABITED, unhealthy.

ILLUSTRATE, illuminate.

IMBIBITION, saturation, steeping.

IMBROCATA, fencing term: a thrust in tierce.

IMPAIR, impairment.

IMPART, give money.

IMPARTER, any one ready to be cheated and to part with his money.

IMPEACH, damage.

IMPERTINENCIES, irrelevancies.

IMPERTINENT(LY), irrelevant(ly), without reason or purpose.

IMPOSITION, duty imposed by.

IMPOTENTLY, beyond power of control.

IMPRESS, money in advance.

IMPULSION, incitement.

IN AND IN, a game played by two or three persons with four dice.

INCENSE, incite, stir up.

INCERATION, act of covering with wax; or reducing a substance to softness of wax.

INCH, "to their—es," according to their stature, capabilities.

INCH-PIN, sweet-bread.

INCONVENIENCE, inconsistency, absurdity.

INCONY, delicate, rare (used as a term of affection).

INCUBEE, incubus.

INCUBUS, evil spirit that oppresses us in sleep, nightmare.

INCURIOUS, unfastidious, uncritical.

INDENT, enter into engagement.

INDIFFERENT, tolerable, passable.

INDIGESTED, shapeless, chaotic.

INDUCE, introduce.

INDUE, supply.

INEXORABLE, relentless.

INFANTED, born, produced.

INFLAME, augment charge.

INGENIOUS, used indiscriminantly for ingenuous; intelligent, talented.

INGENUITY, ingenuousness.

INGENUOUS, generous.

INGINE. See Engin.

INGINER, engineer. (See Enginer).

INGLE, OR ENGHLE, bosom friend, intimate, minion.

INHABITABLE, uninhabitable.

INJURY, insult, affront.

IN-MATE, resident, indwelling.

INNATE, natural.

INNOCENT, simpleton.

INQUEST, jury, or other official body of inquiry.

INQUISITION, inquiry.

INSTANT, immediate.

INSTRUMENT, legal document.

INSURE, assure.

INTEGRATE, complete, perfect.

INTELLIGENCE, secret information, news.

INTEND, note carefully, attend, give ear to, be occupied with.

INTENDMENT, intention.

INTENT, intention, wish.

INTENTION, concentration of attention or gaze.

INTENTIVE, attentive.

INTERESSED, implicated.

INTRUDE, bring in forcibly or without leave.

INVINCIBLY, invisibly.

INWARD, intimate.

IRPE (uncertain), "a fantastic grimace, or contortion of the body: (Gifford)."

JACK, Jack o' the clock, automaton figure that strikes the hour; Jack-a-lent, puppet thrown at in Lent.

JACK, key of a virginal.

JACOB'S STAFF, an instrument for taking altitudes and distances.

JADE, befool.

JEALOUSY, JEALOUS, suspicion, suspicious.

JERKING, lashing.

JEW'S TRUMP, Jew's harp.

JIG, merry ballad or tune; a fanciful dialogue or light comic act introduced at the end or during an interlude of a play.

JOINED (JOINT)-STOOL, folding stool.

JOLL, jowl.

JOLTHEAD, blockhead.

JUMP, agree, tally.

JUST YEAR, no one was capable of the consulship until he was forty-three.

KELL, cocoon.

KELLY, an alchemist.

KEMB, comb.

KEMIA, vessel for distillation.

KIBE, chap, sore.

KILDERKIN, small barrel.

KILL, kiln.

KIND, nature; species; "do one's—," act according to one's nature.

KIRTLE, woman's gown of jacket and petticoat.

KISS OR DRINK AFORE ME, "this is a familiar expression, employed when what the speaker is just about to say is anticipated by another" (Gifford).

KIT, fiddle.

KNACK, snap, click.

KNIPPER-DOLING, a well-known Anabaptist.

KNITTING CUP, marriage cup.

KNOCKING, striking, weighty.

KNOT, company, band; a sandpiper or robin snipe (Tringa canutus); flower-bed laid out in fanciful design.

KURSINED, KYRSIN, christened.

LABOURED, wrought with labour and care.

LADE, load(ed).

LADING, load.

LAID, plotted.

LANCE-KNIGHT (Lanzknecht), a German mercenary foot-soldier.

LAP, fold.

LAR, household god.

LARD, garnish.

LARGE, abundant.

LARUM, alarum, call to arms.

LATTICE, tavern windows were furnished with lattices of various colours.

LAUNDER, to wash gold in aqua regia, so as imperceptibly to extract some of it.

LAVE, ladle, bale.

LAW, "give—," give a start (term of chase).

LAXATIVE, loose.

LAY ABOARD, run alongside generally with intent to board.

LEAGUER, siege, or camp of besieging army.

LEASING, lying.

LEAVE, leave off, desist.

LEER, leering or "empty, hence, perhaps, leer horse, a horse without a rider; leer is an adjective meaning uncontrolled, hence 'leer drunkards'" (Halliwell); according to Nares, a leer (empty) horse meant also a led horse; leeward, left.

LEESE, lose.

LEGS, "make—," do obeisance.

LEIGER, resident representative.

LEIGERITY, legerdemain.

LEMMA, subject proposed, or title of the epigram.

LENTER, slower.

LET, hinder.

LET, hindrance.

LEVEL COIL, a rough game... in which one hunted another from his seat. Hence used for any noisy riot (Halliwell).

LEWD, ignorant.

LEYSTALLS, receptacles of filth.

LIBERAL, ample.

LIEGER, ledger, register.

LIFT(ING), steal(ing); theft.

LIGHT, alight.

LIGHTLY, commonly, usually, often.

LIKE, please.

LIKELY, agreeable, pleasing.

LIME-HOUND, leash-, blood-hound.

LIMMER, vile, worthless.

LIN, leave off.

Line, "by—," by rule.

LINSTOCK, staff to stick in the ground, with forked head to hold a lighted match for firing cannon.

LIQUID, clear.

LIST, listen, hark; like, please.

LIVERY, legal term, delivery of the possession, etc.

LOGGET, small log, stick.

LOOSE, solution; upshot, issue; release of an arrow.

LOSE, give over, desist from; waste.

LOUTING, bowing, cringing.

LUCULENT, bright of beauty.

LUDGATHIANS, dealers on Ludgate Hill.

LURCH, rob, cheat.

LUTE, to close a vessel with some kind of cement.

MACK, unmeaning expletive.

MADGE-HOWLET or OWL, barn-owl.

MAIM, hurt, injury.

MAIN, chief concern (used as a quibble on heraldic term for "hand").

MAINPRISE, becoming surety for a prisoner so as to procure his release.

MAINTENANCE, giving aid, or abetting.

MAKE, mate.

MAKE, MADE, acquaint with business, prepare(d), instruct(ed).

MALLANDERS, disease of horses.

MALT HORSE, dray horse.

MAMMET, puppet.

MAMMOTHREPT, spoiled child.

MANAGE, control (term used for breaking-in horses); handling, administration.

MANGO, slave-dealer.

MANGONISE, polish up for sale.

MANIPLES, bundles, handfuls.

MANKIND, masculine, like a virago.

MANKIND, humanity.

MAPLE FACE, spotted face (N.E.D.).

MARCHPANE, a confection of almonds, sugar, etc.

MARK, "fly to the—," "generally said of a goshawk when, having 'put in' a covey of partridges, she takes stand, marking the spot where they disappeared from view until the falconer arrives to put them out to her" (Harting, Bibl. Accip. Gloss. 226).

MARLE, marvel.

MARROW-BONE MAN, one often on his knees for prayer.

MARRY! exclamation derived from the Virgin's name.

MARRY GIP, "probably originated from By Mary Gipcy" = St. Mary of Egypt, (N.E.D.).

MARTAGAN, Turk's cap lily.

MARYHINCHCO, stringhalt.

MASORETH, Masora, correct form of the scriptural text according to Hebrew tradition.

MASS, abb. for master.

MAUND, beg.

MAUTHER, girl, maid.

MEAN, moderation.

MEASURE, dance, more especially a stately one.

MEAT, "carry—in one's mouth," be a source of money or entertainment.

MEATH, metheglin.

MECHANICAL, belonging to mechanics, mean, vulgar.

MEDITERRANEO, middle aisle of St. Paul's, a general resort for business and amusement.

MEET WITH, even with.

MELICOTTON, a late kind of peach.

MENSTRUE, solvent.

MERCAT, market.

MERD, excrement.

MERE, undiluted; absolute, unmitigated.

MESS, party of four.

METHEGLIN, fermented liquor, of which one ingredient was honey.

METOPOSCOPY, study of physiognomy.

MIDDLING GOSSIP, go-between.

MIGNIARD, dainty, delicate.

MILE-END, training-ground of the city.

MINE-MEN, sappers.

MINION, form of cannon.

MINSITIVE, (?) mincing, affected (N.E.D.).

MISCELLANY MADAM, "a female trader in miscellaneous articles; a dealer in trinkets or ornaments of various kinds, such as kept shops in the New Exchange" (Nares).

MISCELLINE, mixed grain; medley.

MISCONCEIT, misconception.

MISPRISE, MISPRISION, mistake, misunderstanding.

MISTAKE AWAY, carry away as if by mistake.

MITHRIDATE, an antidote against poison.

MOCCINIGO, small Venetian coin, worth about ninepence.

MODERN, in the mode; ordinary, commonplace.

MOMENT, force or influence of value.

MONTANTO, upward stroke.

MONTH'S MIND, violent desire.

MOORISH, like a moor or waste.

MORGLAY, sword of Bevis of Southampton.

MORRICE-DANCE, dance on May Day, etc., in which certain personages were represented.

MORTALITY, death.

MORT-MAL, old sore, gangrene.

MOSCADINO, confection flavoured with musk.

MOTHER, Hysterica passio.

MOTION, proposal, request; puppet, puppet-show; "one of the small figures on the face of a large clock which was moved by the vibration of the pendulum" (Whalley).

MOTION, suggest, propose.

MOTLEY, parti-coloured dress of a fool; hence used to signify pertaining to, or like, a fool.

MOTTE, motto.

MOURNIVAL, set of four aces or court cards in a hand; a quartette.

MOW, setord hay or sheaves of grain.

MUCH! expressive of irony and incredulity.

MUCKINDER, handkerchief.

MULE, "born to ride on—," judges or serjeants-at-law formerly rode on mules when going in state to Westminster (Whally).

MULLETS, small pincers.

MUM-CHANCE, game of chance, played in silence.

MUN, must.

MUREY, dark crimson red.

MUSCOVY-GLASS, mica.

MUSE, wonder.

MUSICAL, in harmony.

MUSS, mouse; scramble.

MYROBOLANE, foreign conserve, "a dried plum, brought from the Indies."

MYSTERY, art, trade, profession.

NAIL, "to the—" (ad unguem), to perfection, to the very utmost.

NATIVE, natural.

NEAT, cattle.

NEAT, smartly apparelled; unmixed; dainty.

NEATLY, neatly finished.

NEATNESS, elegance.

NEIS, nose, scent.

NEUF (NEAF, NEIF), fist.

NEUFT, newt.

NIAISE, foolish, inexperienced person.

NICE, fastidious, trivial, finical, scrupulous.

NICENESS, fastidiousness.

NICK, exact amount; right moment; "set in the—," meaning uncertain.

NICE, suit, fit; hit, seize the right moment, etc., exactly hit on, hit off.

NOBLE, gold coin worth 6s. 8d.

NOCENT, harmful.

NIL, not will.

NOISE, company of musicians.

NOMENTACK, an Indian chief from Virginia.

NONES, nonce.

NOTABLE, egregious.

NOTE, sign, token.

NOUGHT, "be—," go to the devil, be hanged, etc.

NOWT-HEAD, blockhead.

NUMBER, rhythm.

NUPSON, oaf, simpleton.

OADE, woad.

OBARNI, preparation of mead.

OBJECT, oppose; expose; interpose.

OBLATRANT, barking, railing.

OBNOXIOUS, liable, exposed; offensive.

OBSERVANCE, homage, devoted service.

OBSERVANT, attentive, obsequious.

OBSERVE, show deference, respect.

OBSERVER, one who shows deference, or waits upon another.

OBSTANCY, legal phrase, "juridical opposition."

OBSTREPEROUS, clamorous, vociferous.

OBSTUPEFACT, stupefied.

ODLING, (?) "must have some relation to tricking and cheating" (Nares).

OMINOUS, deadly, fatal.

ONCE, at once; for good and all; used also for additional emphasis.

ONLY, pre-eminent, special.

OPEN, make public; expound.

OPPILATION, obstruction.

OPPONE, oppose.

OPPOSITE, antagonist.

OPPRESS, suppress.

ORIGINOUS, native.

ORT, remnant, scrap.

OUT, "to be—," to have forgotten one's part; not at one with each other.

OUTCRY, sale by auction.

OUTRECUIDANCE, arrogance, presumption.

OUTSPEAK, speak more than.

OVERPARTED, given too difficult a part to play.

OWLSPIEGEL. See Howleglass.

OYEZ! (O YES!), hear ye! call of the public crier when about to make a proclamation.

PACKING PENNY, "give a—," dismiss, send packing.

PAD, highway.

PAD-HORSE, road-horse.

PAINED (PANED) SLOPS, full breeches made of strips of different colour and material.

PAINFUL, diligent, painstaking.

PAINT, blush.

PALINODE, ode of recantation.

PALL, weaken, dim, make stale.

PALM, triumph.

PAN, skirt of dress or coat.

PANNEL, pad, or rough kind of saddle.

PANNIER-ALLY, inhabited by tripe-sellers.

PANNIER-MAN, hawker; a man employed about the inns of court to bring in provisions, set the table, etc.

PANTOFLE, indoor shoe, slipper.

PARAMENTOS, fine trappings.

PARANOMASIE, a play upon words.

PARANTORY, (?) peremptory.

PARCEL, particle, fragment (used contemptuously); article.

PARCEL, part, partly.

PARCEL-POET, poetaster.

PARERGA, subordinate matters.

PARGET, to paint or plaster the face.

PARLE, parley.

PARLOUS, clever, shrewd.

PART, apportion.

PARTAKE, participate in.

PARTED, endowed, talented.

PARTICULAR, individual person.

PARTIZAN, kind of halberd.

PARTRICH, partridge.

PARTS, qualities, endowments.

PASH, dash, smash.

PASS, care, trouble oneself.

PASSADO, fencing term: a thrust.

PASSAGE, game at dice.

PASSINGLY, exceedingly.

PASSION, effect caused by external agency.

PASSION, "in—," in so melancholy a tone, so pathetically.

PATOUN, (?) Fr. Paton, pellet of dough; perhaps the "moulding of the tobacco... for the pipe" (Gifford); (?) variant of Petun, South American name of tobacco.

PATRICO, the recorder, priest, orator of strolling beggars or gipsies.

PATTEN, shoe with wooden sole; "go—," keep step with, accompany.

PAUCA VERBA, few words.

PAVIN, a stately dance.

PEACE, "with my master's—," by leave, favour.

PECULIAR, individual, single.

PEDANT, teacher of the languages.

PEEL, baker's shovel.

PEEP, speak in a small or shrill voice.

PEEVISH(LY), foolish(ly), capricious(ly); childish(ly).

PELICAN, a retort fitted with tube or tubes, for continuous distillation.

PENCIL, small tuft of hair.

PERDUE, soldier accustomed to hazardous service.

PEREMPTORY, resolute, bold; imperious; thorough, utter, absolute(ly).

PERIMETER, circumference of a figure.

PERIOD, limit, end.

PERK, perk up.

PERPETUANA, "this seems to be that glossy kind of stuff now called everlasting, and anciently worn by serjeants and other city officers" (Gifford).

PERSPECTIVE, a view, scene or scenery; an optical device which gave a distortion to the picture unless seen from a particular point; a relief, modelled to produce an optical illusion.

PERSPICIL, optic glass.

PERSTRINGE, criticise, censure.

PERSUADE, inculcate, commend.

PERSWAY, mitigate.

PERTINACY, pertinacity.

PESTLING, pounding, pulverising, like a pestle.

PETASUS, broad-brimmed hat or winged cap worn by Mercury.

PETITIONARY, supplicatory.

PETRONEL, a kind of carbine or light gun carried by horsemen.

PETULANT, pert, insolent.

PHERE. See Fere.

PHLEGMA, watery distilled liquor (old chem. "water").

PHRENETIC, madman.

PICARDIL, stiff upright collar fastened on to the coat (Whalley).

PICT-HATCH, disreputable quarter of London.

PIECE, person, used for woman or girl; a gold coin worth in Jonson's time 20s. or 22s.

PIECES OF EIGHT, Spanish coin: piastre equal to eight reals.

PIED, variegated.

PIE-POUDRES (Fr. pied-poudreux, dusty-foot), court held at fairs to administer justice to itinerant vendors and buyers.

PILCHER, term of contempt; one who wore a buff or leather jerkin, as did the serjeants of the counter; a pilferer.

PILED, pilled, peeled, bald.

PILL'D, polled, fleeced.

PIMLICO, "sometimes spoken of as a person—perhaps master of a house famous for a particular ale" (Gifford).

PINE, afflict, distress.

PINK, stab with a weapon; pierce or cut in scallops for ornament.

PINNACE, a go-between in infamous sense.

PISMIRE, ant.

PISTOLET, gold coin, worth about 6s.

PITCH, height of a bird of prey's flight.

PLAGUE, punishment, torment.

PLAIN, lament.

PLAIN SONG, simple melody.

PLAISE, plaice.

PLANET, "struck with a—," planets were supposed to have powers of blasting or exercising secret influences.

PLAUSIBLE, pleasing.

PLAUSIBLY, approvingly.

PLOT, plan.

PLY, apply oneself to.

POESIE, posy, motto inside a ring.

POINT IN HIS DEVICE, exact in every particular.

POINTS, tagged laces or cords for fastening the breeches to the doublet.

POINT-TRUSSER, one who trussed (tied) his master's points (q.v.).

POISE, weigh, balance.

POKING-STICK, stick used for setting the plaits of ruffs.

POLITIC, politician.

POLITIC, judicious, prudent, political.

POLITICIAN, plotter, intriguer.

POLL, strip, plunder, gain by extortion.

POMANDER, ball of perfume, worn or hung about the person to prevent infection, or for foppery.

POMMADO, vaulting on a horse without the aid of stirrups.

PONTIC, sour.

POPULAR, vulgar, of the populace.

POPULOUS, numerous.

PORT, gate; print of a deer's foot.

PORT, transport.

PORTAGUE, Portuguese gold coin, worth over 3 or 4 pounds.

PORTCULLIS, "—of coin," some old coins have a portcullis stamped on their reverse (Whalley).

PORTENT, marvel, prodigy; sinister omen.

PORTENTOUS, prophesying evil, threatening.

PORTER, references appear "to allude to Parsons, the king's porter, who was... near seven feet high" (Whalley).

POSSESS, inform, acquaint.

POST AND PAIR, a game at cards.

POSY, motto. (See Poesie).

POTCH, poach.

POULT-FOOT, club-foot.

POUNCE, claw, talon.

PRACTICE, intrigue, concerted plot.

PRACTISE, plot, conspire.

PRAGMATIC, an expert, agent.

PRAGMATIC, officious, conceited, meddling.

PRECEDENT, record of proceedings.

PRECEPT, warrant, summons.

PRECISIAN(ISM), Puritan(ism), preciseness.

PREFER, recommend.

PRESENCE, presence chamber.

PRESENT(LY), immediate(ly), without delay; at the present time; actually.

PRESS, force into service.

PREST, ready.

PRETEND, assert, allege.

PREVENT, anticipate.

PRICE, worth, excellence.

PRICK, point, dot used in the writing of Hebrew and other languages.

PRICK, prick out, mark off, select; trace, track; "—away," make off with speed.

PRIMERO, game of cards.

PRINCOX, pert boy.

PRINT, "in—," to the letter, exactly.

PRISTINATE, former.

PRIVATE, private interests.

PRIVATE, privy, intimate.

PROCLIVE, prone to.

PRODIGIOUS, monstrous, unnatural.

PRODIGY, monster.

PRODUCED, prolonged.

PROFESS, pretend.

PROJECTION, the throwing of the "powder of projection" into the crucible to turn the melted metal into gold or silver.

PROLATE, pronounce drawlingly.

PROPER, of good appearance, handsome; own, particular.

PROPERTIES, stage necessaries.

PROPERTY, duty; tool.

PRORUMPED, burst out.

PROTEST, vow, proclaim (an affected word of that time); formally declare non-payment, etc., of bill of exchange; fig. failure of personal credit, etc.

PROVANT, soldier's allowance—hence, of common make.

PROVIDE, foresee.

PROVIDENCE, foresight, prudence.

PUBLICATION, making a thing public of common property (N.E.D.).

PUCKFIST, puff-ball; insipid, insignificant, boasting fellow.

PUFF-WING, shoulder puff.

PUISNE, judge of inferior rank, a junior.

PULCHRITUDE, beauty.

PUMP, shoe.

PUNGENT, piercing.

PUNTO, point, hit.

PURCEPT, precept, warrant.

PURE, fine, capital, excellent.

PURELY, perfectly, utterly.

PURL, pleat or fold of a ruff.

PURSE-NET, net of which the mouth is drawn together with a string.

PURSUIVANT, state messenger who summoned the persecuted seminaries; warrant officer.

PURSY, PURSINESS, shortwinded(ness).

PUT, make a push, exert yourself (N.E.D.).

PUT OFF, excuse, shift.

PUT ON, incite, encourage; proceed with, take in hand, try.

QUACKSALVER, quack.

QUAINT, elegant, elaborated, ingenious, clever.

QUAR, quarry.

QUARRIED, seized, or fed upon, as prey.

QUEAN, hussy, jade.

QUEASY, hazardous, delicate.

QUELL, kill, destroy.

QUEST, request; inquiry.

QUESTION, decision by force of arms.

QUESTMAN, one appointed to make official inquiry.

QUIB, QUIBLIN, quibble, quip.

QUICK, the living.

QUIDDIT, quiddity, legal subtlety.

QUIRK, clever turn or trick.

QUIT, requite, repay; acquit, absolve; rid; forsake, leave.

QUITTER-BONE, disease of horses.

QUODLING, codling.

QUOIT, throw like a quoit, chuck.

QUOTE, take note, observe, write down.

RACK, neck of mutton or pork (Halliwell).

RAKE UP, cover over.

RAMP, rear, as a lion, etc.

RAPT, carry away.

RAPT, enraptured.

RASCAL, young or inferior deer.

RASH, strike with a glancing oblique blow, as a boar with its tusk.

RATSEY, GOMALIEL, a famous highwayman.

RAVEN, devour.

REACH, understand.

REAL, regal.

REBATU, ruff, turned-down collar.

RECTOR, RECTRESS, director, governor.

REDARGUE, confute.

REDUCE, bring back.

REED, rede, counsel, advice.

REEL, run riot.

REFEL, refute.

REFORMADOES, disgraced or disbanded soldiers.

REGIMENT, government.

REGRESSION, return.

REGULAR ("Tale of a Tub"), regular noun (quibble) (N.E.D.).

RELIGION, "make—of," make a point of, scruple of.

RELISH, savour.

REMNANT, scrap of quotation.

REMORA, species of fish.

RENDER, depict, exhibit, show.

REPAIR, reinstate.

REPETITION, recital, narration.

REREMOUSE, bat.

RESIANT, resident.

RESIDENCE, sediment.

RESOLUTION, judgment, decision.

RESOLVE, inform; assure; prepare, make up one's mind; dissolve; come to a decision, be convinced; relax, set at ease.

RESPECTIVE, worthy of respect; regardful, discriminative.

RESPECTIVELY, with reverence.

RESPECTLESS, regardless.

RESPIRE, exhale; inhale.

RESPONSIBLE, correspondent.

REST, musket-rest.

REST, "set up one's—," venture one's all, one's last stake (from game of primero).

REST, arrest.

RESTIVE, RESTY, dull, inactive.

RETCHLESS(NESS), reckless(ness).

RETIRE, cause to retire.

RETRICATO, fencing term.

RETRIEVE, rediscovery of game once sprung.

RETURNS, ventures sent abroad, for the safe return of which so much money is received.

REVERBERATE, dissolve or blend by reflected heat.

REVERSE, REVERSO, back-handed thrust, etc., in fencing.

REVISE, reconsider a sentence.

RHEUM, spleen, caprice.

RIBIBE, abusive term for an old woman.

RID, destroy, do away with.

RIFLING, raffling, dicing.

RING, "cracked within the—," coins so cracked were unfit for currency.

RISSE, risen, rose.

RIVELLED, wrinkled.

ROARER, swaggerer.

ROCHET, fish of the gurnet kind.

ROCK, distaff.

RODOMONTADO, braggadocio.

ROGUE, vagrant, vagabond.

RONDEL, "a round mark in the score of a public-house" (Nares); roundel.

ROOK, sharper; fool, dupe.

ROSAKER, similar to ratsbane.

ROSA-SOLIS, a spiced spirituous liquor.

ROSES, rosettes.

ROUND, "gentlemen of the—," officers of inferior rank.

ROUND TRUNKS, trunk hose, short loose breeches reaching almost or quite to the knees.

ROUSE, carouse, bumper.

ROVER, arrow used for shooting at a random mark at uncertain distance.

ROWLY-POWLY, roly-poly.

RUDE, RUDENESS, unpolished, rough(ness), coarse(ness).

RUFFLE, flaunt, swagger.

RUG, coarse frieze.

RUG-GOWNS, gown made of rug.

RUSH, reference to rushes with which the floors were then strewn.

RUSHER, one who strewed the floor with rushes.

RUSSET, homespun cloth of neutral or reddish-brown colour.

SACK, loose, flowing gown.

SADLY, seriously, with gravity.

SAD(NESS), sober, serious(ness).

SAFFI, bailiffs.

ST. THOMAS A WATERINGS, place in Surrey where criminals were executed.

SAKER, small piece of ordnance.

SALT, leap.

SALT, lascivious.

SAMPSUCHINE, sweet marjoram.

SARABAND, a slow dance.

SATURNALS, began December 17.

SAUCINESS, presumption, insolence.

SAUCY, bold, impudent, wanton.

SAUNA (Lat.), a gesture of contempt.

SAVOUR, perceive; gratify, please; to partake of the nature.

SAY, sample.

SAY, assay, try.

SCALD, word of contempt, implying dirt and disease.

SCALLION, shalot, small onion.

SCANDERBAG, "name which the Turks (in allusion to Alexander the Great) gave to the brave Castriot, chief of Albania, with whom they had continual wars. His romantic life had just been translated" (Gifford).

SCAPE, escape.

SCARAB, beetle.

SCARTOCCIO, fold of paper, cover, cartouch, cartridge.

SCONCE, head.

SCOPE, aim.

SCOT AND LOT, tax, contribution (formerly a parish assessment).

SCOTOMY, dizziness in the head.

SCOUR, purge.

SCOURSE, deal, swap.

SCRATCHES, disease of horses.

SCROYLE, mean, rascally fellow.

SCRUPLE, doubt.

SEAL, put hand to the giving up of property or rights.

SEALED, stamped as genuine.

SEAM-RENT, ragged.

SEAMING LACES, insertion or edging.

SEAR UP, close by searing, burning.

SEARCED, sifted.

SECRETARY, able to keep a secret.

SECULAR, worldly, ordinary, commonplace.

SECURE, confident.

SEELIE, happy, blest.

SEISIN, legal term: possession.

SELLARY, lewd person.

SEMBLABLY, similarly.

SEMINARY, a Romish priest educated in a foreign seminary.

SENSELESS, insensible, without sense or feeling.

SENSIBLY, perceptibly.

SENSIVE, sensitive.

SENSUAL, pertaining to the physical or material.

SERENE, harmful dew of evening.

SERICON, red tincture.

SERVANT, lover.

SERVICES, doughty deeds of arms.

SESTERCE, Roman copper coin.

SET, stake, wager.

SET UP, drill.

SETS, deep plaits of the ruff.

SEWER, officer who served up the feast, and brought water for the hands of the guests.

SHAPE, a suit by way of disguise.

SHIFT, fraud, dodge.

SHIFTER, cheat.

SHITTLE, shuttle; "shittle-cock," shuttlecock.

SHOT, tavern reckoning.

SHOT-CLOG, one only tolerated because he paid the shot (reckoning) for the rest.

SHOT-FREE, scot-free, not having to pay.

SHOVE-GROAT, low kind of gambling amusement, perhaps somewhat of the nature of pitch and toss.

SHOT-SHARKS, drawers.

SHREWD, mischievous, malicious, curst.

SHREWDLY, keenly, in a high degree.

SHRIVE, sheriff; posts were set up before his door for proclamations, or to indicate his residence.

SHROVING, Shrovetide, season of merriment.

SIGILLA, seal, mark.

SILENCED BRETHERN, MINISTERS, those of the Church or Nonconformists who had been silenced, deprived, etc.

SILLY, simple, harmless.

SIMPLE, silly, witless; plain, true.

SIMPLES, herbs.

SINGLE, term of chase, signifying when the hunted stag is separated from the herd, or forced to break covert.

SINGLE, weak, silly.

SINGLE-MONEY, small change.

SINGULAR, unique, supreme.

SI-QUIS, bill, advertisement.

SKELDRING, getting money under false pretences; swindling.

SKILL, "it—s not," matters not.

SKINK(ER), pour, draw(er), tapster.

SKIRT, tail.

SLEEK, smooth.

SLICE, fire shovel or pan (dial.).

SLICK, sleek, smooth.

'SLID, 'SLIGHT, 'SPRECIOUS, irreverent oaths.

SLIGHT, sleight, cunning, cleverness; trick.

SLIP, counterfeit coin, bastard.

SLIPPERY, polished and shining.

SLOPS, large loose breeches.

SLOT, print of a stag's foot.

SLUR, put a slur on; cheat (by sliding a die in some way).

SMELT, gull, simpleton.

SNORLE, "perhaps snarl, as Puppy is addressed" (Cunningham).

SNOTTERIE, filth.

SNUFF, anger, resentment; "take in—," take offence at.

SNUFFERS, small open silver dishes for holding snuff, or receptacle for placing snuffers in (Halliwell).

SOCK, shoe worn by comic actors.

SOD, seethe.

SOGGY, soaked, sodden.

SOIL, "take—," said of a hunted stag when he takes to the water for safety.

SOL, sou.

SOLDADOES, soldiers.

SOLICIT, rouse, excite to action.

SOOTH, flattery, cajolery.

SOOTHE, flatter, humour.

SOPHISTICATE, adulterate.

SORT, company, party; rank, degree.

SORT, suit, fit; select.

SOUSE, ear.

SOUSED ("Devil is an Ass"), fol. read "sou't," which Dyce interprets as "a variety of the spelling of "shu'd": to "shu" is to scare a bird away." (See his "Webster," page 350).

SOWTER, cobbler.

SPAGYRICA, chemistry according to the teachings of Paracelsus.

SPAR, bar.

SPEAK, make known, proclaim.

SPECULATION, power of sight.

SPED, to have fared well, prospered.

SPEECE, species.

SPIGHT, anger, rancour.

SPINNER, spider.

SPINSTRY, lewd person.

SPITTLE, hospital, lazar-house.

SPLEEN, considered the seat of the emotions.

SPLEEN, caprice, humour, mood.

SPRUNT, spruce.

SPURGE, foam.

SPUR-RYAL, gold coin worth 15s.

SQUIRE, square, measure; "by the—," exactly.

STAGGERING, wavering, hesitating.

STAIN, disparagement, disgrace.

STALE, decoy, or cover, stalking-horse.

STALE, make cheap, common.

STALK, approach stealthily or under cover.

STALL, forestall.

STANDARD, suit.

STAPLE, market, emporium.

STARK, downright.

STARTING-HOLES, loopholes of escape.

STATE, dignity; canopied chair of state; estate.

STATUMINATE, support vines by poles or stakes; used by Pliny (Gifford).

STAY, gag.

STAY, await; detain.

STICKLER, second or umpire.

STIGMATISE, mark, brand.

STILL, continual(ly), constant(ly).

STINKARD, stinking fellow.

STINT, stop.

STIPTIC, astringent.

STOCCATA, thrust in fencing.

STOCK-FISH, salted and dried fish.

STOMACH, pride, valour.

STOMACH, resent.

STOOP, swoop down as a hawk.

STOP, fill, stuff.

STOPPLE, stopper.

STOTE, stoat, weasel.

STOUP, stoop, swoop=bow.

STRAIGHT, straightway.

STRAMAZOUN (Ital. stramazzone), a down blow, as opposed to the thrust.

STRANGE, like a stranger, unfamiliar.

STRANGENESS, distance of behaviour.

STREIGHTS, OR BERMUDAS, labyrinth of alleys and courts in the Strand.

STRIGONIUM, Grau in Hungary, taken from the Turks in 1597.

STRIKE, balance (accounts).

STRINGHALT, disease of horses.

STROKER, smoother, flatterer.

STROOK, p.p. of "strike."

STRUMMEL-PATCHED, strummel is glossed in dialect dicts. as "a long, loose and dishevelled head of hair."

STUDIES, studious efforts.

STYLE, title; pointed instrument used for writing on wax tablets.

SUBTLE, fine, delicate, thin; smooth, soft.

SUBTLETY (SUBTILITY), subtle device.

SUBURB, connected with loose living.

SUCCUBAE, demons in form of women.

SUCK, extract money from.

SUFFERANCE, suffering.

SUMMED, term of falconry: with full-grown plumage.

SUPER-NEGULUM, topers turned the cup bottom up when it was empty.

SUPERSTITIOUS, over-scrupulous.

SUPPLE, to make pliant.

SURBATE, make sore with walking.

SURCEASE, cease.

SUR-REVERENCE, save your reverence.

SURVISE, peruse.

SUSCITABILITY, excitability.

SUSPECT, suspicion.

SUSPEND, suspect.

SUSPENDED, held over for the present.

SUTLER, victualler.

SWAD, clown, boor.

SWATH BANDS, swaddling clothes.

SWINGE, beat.

TABERD, emblazoned mantle or tunic worn by knights and heralds.

TABLE(S), "pair of—," tablets, note-book.

TABOR, small drum.

TABRET, tabor.

TAFFETA, silk; "tuft-taffeta," a more costly silken fabric.

TAINT, "—a staff," break a lance at tilting in an unscientific or dishonourable manner.

TAKE IN, capture, subdue.

TAKE ME WITH YOU, let me understand you.

TAKE UP, obtain on credit, borrow.

TALENT, sum or weight of Greek currency.

TALL, stout, brave.

TANKARD-BEARERS, men employed to fetch water from the conduits.

TARLETON, celebrated comedian and jester.

TARTAROUS, like a Tartar.

TAVERN-TOKEN, "to swallow a—," get drunk.

TELL, count.

TELL-TROTH, truth-teller.

TEMPER, modify, soften.

TENDER, show regard, care for, cherish; manifest.

TENT, "take—," take heed.

TERSE, swept and polished.

TERTIA, "that portion of an army levied out of one particular district or division of a country" (Gifford).

TESTON, tester, coin worth 6d.

THIRDBOROUGH, constable.

THREAD, quality.

THREAVES, droves.

THREE-FARTHINGS, piece of silver current under Elizabeth.

THREE-PILED, of finest quality, exaggerated.

THRIFTILY, carefully.

THRUMS, ends of the weaver's warp; coarse yarn made from.

THUMB-RING, familiar spirits were supposed capable of being carried about in various ornaments or parts of dress.

TIBICINE, player on the tibia, or pipe.

TICK-TACK, game similar to backgammon.

TIGHTLY, promptly.

TIM, (?) expressive of a climax of nonentity.

TIMELESS, untimely, unseasonable.

TINCTURE, an essential or spiritual principle supposed by alchemists to be transfusible into material things; an imparted characteristic or tendency.

TINK, tinkle.

TIPPET, "turn—," change behaviour or way of life.

TIPSTAFF, staff tipped with metal.

TIRE, head-dress.

TIRE, feed ravenously, like a bird of prey.

TITILLATION, that which tickles the senses, as a perfume.

TOD, fox.

TOILED, worn out, harassed.

TOKEN, piece of base metal used in place of very small coin, when this was scarce.

TONNELS, nostrils.

TOP, "parish—," large top kept in villages for amusement and exercise in frosty weather when people were out of work.

TOTER, tooter, player on a wind instrument.

TOUSE, pull, rend.

TOWARD, docile, apt; on the way to; as regards, present, at hand.

TOY, whim; trick; term of contempt.

TRACT, attraction.

TRAIN, allure, entice.

TRANSITORY, transmittable.

TRANSLATE, transform.

TRAY-TRIP, game at dice (success depended on throwing a three) (Nares).

TREACHOUR (TRECHER), traitor.

TREEN, wooden.

TRENCHER, serving-man who carved or served food.

TRENDLE-TAIL, trundle-tail, curly-tailed.

TRICK (TRICKING), term of heraldry: to draw outline of coat of arms, etc., without blazoning.

TRIG, a spruce, dandified man.

TRILL, trickle.

TRILLIBUB, tripe, any worthless, trifling thing.

TRIPOLY, "come from—," able to perform feats of agility, a "jest nominal," depending on the first part of the word (Gifford).

TRITE, worn, shabby.

TRIVIA, three-faced goddess (Hecate).

TROJAN, familiar term for an equal or inferior; thief.

TROLL, sing loudly.

TROMP, trump, deceive.

TROPE, figure of speech.

TROW, think, believe, wonder.

TROWLE, troll.

TROWSES, breeches, drawers.

TRUCHMAN, interpreter.

TRUNDLE, JOHN, well-known printer.

TRUNDLE, roll, go rolling along.

TRUNDLING CHEATS, term among gipsies and beggars for carts or coaches (Gifford).

TRUNK, speaking-tube.

TRUSS, tie the tagged laces that fastened the breeches to the doublet.

TUBICINE, trumpeter.

TUCKET (Ital. toccato), introductory flourish on the trumpet.

TUITION, guardianship.

TUMBLER, a particular kind of dog so called from the mode of his hunting.

TUMBREL-SLOP, loose, baggy breeches.

TURD, excrement.

TUSK, gnash the teeth (Century Dict.).

TWIRE, peep, twinkle.

TWOPENNY ROOM, gallery.

TYRING-HOUSE, attiring-room.

ULENSPIEGEL. See Howleglass.

UMBRATILE, like or pertaining to a shadow.

UMBRE, brown dye.

UNBATED, unabated.

UNBORED, (?) excessively bored.

UNCARNATE, not fleshly, or of flesh.

UNCOUTH, strange, unusual.

UNDERTAKER, "one who undertook by his influence in the House of Commons to carry things agreeably to his Majesty's wishes" (Whalley); one who becomes surety for.

UNEQUAL, unjust.

UNEXCEPTED, no objection taken at.

UNFEARED, unaffrighted.

UNHAPPILY, unfortunately.

UNICORN'S HORN, supposed antidote to poison.

UNKIND(LY), unnatural(ly).

UNMANNED, untamed (term in falconry).

UNQUIT, undischarged.

UNREADY, undressed.

UNRUDE, rude to an extreme.

UNSEASONED, unseasonable, unripe.

UNSEELED, a hawk's eyes were "seeled" by sewing the eyelids together with fine thread.

UNTIMELY, unseasonably.

UNVALUABLE, invaluable.

UPBRAID, make a matter of reproach.

UPSEE, heavy kind of Dutch beer (Halliwell); "—Dutch," in the Dutch fashion.

UPTAILS ALL, refrain of a popular song.

URGE, allege as accomplice, instigator.

URSHIN, URCHIN, hedgehog.

USE, interest on money; part of sermon dealing with the practical application of doctrine.

USE, be in the habit of, accustomed to; put out to interest.

USQUEBAUGH, whisky.

USURE, usury.

UTTER, put in circulation, make to pass current; put forth for sale.

VAIL, bow, do homage.

VAILS, tips, gratuities.

VALL. See Vail.

VALLIES (Fr. valise), portmanteau, bag.

VAPOUR(S) (n. and v.), used affectedly, like "humour," in many senses, often very vaguely and freely ridiculed by Jonson; humour, disposition, whims, brag(ging), hector(ing), etc.

VARLET, bailiff, or serjeant-at-mace.

VAUT, vault.

VEER (naut.), pay out.

VEGETAL, vegetable; person full of life and vigour.

VELLUTE, velvet.

VELVET CUSTARD. Cf. "Taming of the Shrew," iv. 3, 82, "custard coffin," coffin being the raised crust over a pie.

VENT, vend, sell; give outlet to; scent, snuff up.

VENUE, bout (fencing term).

VERDUGO (Span.), hangman, executioner.

VERGE, "in the—," within a certain distance of the court.

VEX, agitate, torment.

VICE, the buffoon of old moralities; some kind of machinery for moving a puppet (Gifford).

VIE AND REVIE, to hazard a certain sum, and to cover it with a larger one.

VINCENT AGAINST YORK, two heralds-at-arms.

VINDICATE, avenge.

VIRGE, wand, rod.

VIRGINAL, old form of piano.

VIRTUE, valour.

VIVELY, in lifelike manner, livelily.

VIZARD, mask.

VOGUE, rumour, gossip.

VOICE, vote.

VOID, leave, quit.

VOLARY, cage, aviary.

VOLLEY, "at—," "o' the volee," at random (from a term of tennis).

VORLOFFE, furlough.

WADLOE, keeper of the Devil Tavern, where Jonson and his friends met in the 'Apollo' room (Whalley).

WAIGHTS, waits, night musicians, "band of musical watchmen" (Webster), or old form of "hautboys."

WANNION, "vengeance," "plague" (Nares).

WARD, a famous pirate.

WARD, guard in fencing.

WATCHET, pale, sky blue.

WEAL, welfare.

WEED, garment.

WEFT, waif.

WEIGHTS, "to the gold—," to every minute particular.

WELKIN, sky.

WELL-SPOKEN, of fair speech.

WELL-TORNED, turned and polished, as on a wheel.

WELT, hem, border of fur.

WHER, whether.

WHETSTONE, GEORGE, an author who lived 1544(?) to 1587(?).

WHIFF, a smoke, or drink; "taking the—," inhaling the tobacco smoke or some such accomplishment.

WHIGH-HIES, neighings, whinnyings.

WHIMSY, whim, "humour."

WHINILING, (?) whining, weakly.

WHIT, (?) a mere jot.

WHITEMEAT, food made of milk or eggs.

WICKED, bad, clumsy.

WICKER, pliant, agile.

WILDING, esp. fruit of wild apple or crab tree (Webster).

WINE, "I have the—for you," Prov.: I have the perquisites (of the office) which you are to share (Cunningham).

WINNY, "same as old word "wonne," to stay, etc." (Whalley).

WISE-WOMAN, fortune-teller.

WISH, recommend.

WISS (WUSSE), "I—," certainly, of a truth.

WITHOUT, beyond.

WITTY, cunning, ingenious, clever.

WOOD, collection, lot.

WOODCOCK, term of contempt.

WOOLSACK ("—pies"), name of tavern.

WORT, unfermented beer.

WOUNDY, great, extreme.

WREAK, revenge.

WROUGHT, wrought upon.

WUSSE, interjection. (See Wiss).

YEANLING, lamb, kid.

ZANY, an inferior clown, who attended upon the chief fool and mimicked his tricks.

www.ingramcontent.com/pod-product-compliance
Lightning Source LLC
Chambersburg PA
CBHW052005090426
42741CB00008B/1560